Critical Rural Pedagogy

Critical Rural Pedagogy

Connecting College Students with American Literature

Sharon Mitchler
Centralia College

National Council of Teachers of English
340 N. Neil St., Suite #104, Champaign, IL 61820
www.ncte.org

Staff Editor: Cynthia Gomez
Manuscript Editor: Leigh Scarcliff
Interior Design: Jenny Jensen Greenleaf
Cover Design: Beth DeWilde

ISBN (print): 978-0-8141-0090-5
ISBN (epub): 978-0-8141-0091-2
ISBN (PDF): 978-0-8141-0092-9

It is the policy of NCTE in its journals and other publications to provide a forum for the open discussion of ideas concerning the content and the teaching of English and the language arts. Publicity accorded to any particular point of view does not imply endorsement by the Executive Committee, the Board of Directors, or the membership at large, except in announcements of policy, where such endorsement is clearly specified.

NCTE provides equal employment opportunity (EEO) to all staff members and applicants for employment without regard to race, color, religion, sex, national origin, age, physical, mental or perceived handicap/disability, sexual orientation including gender identity or expression, ancestry, genetic information, marital status, military status, unfavorable discharge from military service, pregnancy, citizenship status, personal appearance, matriculation or political affiliation, or any other protected status under applicable federal, state, and local laws.

Every effort has been made to provide current URLs and email addresses, but because of the rapidly changing nature of the web, some sites and addresses may no longer be accessible.

Library of Congress Control Number: 2023002886

For Steve, who made me promise.

Contents

Acknowledgments

This book would not exist without the support of friends and colleagues. In time order, first is James Walton, president of Centralia College, who encouraged the initial vision, approved my sabbatical, approved reassigned time for writing, and mentored me through my doctoral program. Candice Rai stepped in to direct my dissertation with good humor, patience, and astute feedback in all parts of the process. The faculty, staff, and students of Centralia College encouraged me, joining in the fun of "dress until dissertation." Notably, faculty members Jody Peterson, Steve Norton, and Susanne Weil listened to my worries for hours in their offices and gave thoughtful advice at every crisis point.

The English department graduate students from my cohort have cheered me on through first the dissertation and then manuscript creation. Michelle LaFrance, Heather Hill, Jennifer LeMesurier, and Ed Chang shared their expertise even as they moved on to their new academic homes across the United States. Stephanie Kerschbaum's invitation to join a group for first academic book writers during the pandemic kept me connected to this work despite the challenges of suddenly teaching community college students remotely. Finally, Jenny Lambe, Sarah Singer, Ben Stanley, Elliot Tetreault, and I have met weekly over Zoom to puzzle through the process of publishing in academia. Their empathetic wisdom has kept me writing.

Prologue

This book began as a dissertation, which I finished in March of 2015, and then put away expecting to come back to it in the summer. Summer came and went, and before I realized it five years had passed. But in the supercharged political intensity of the COVID-19 year of 2020, I began to recognize that the heart of this book was not only important, it was also needed. At a time of such a divisive urban-rural split, this book proposes using a pedagogical approach that ensures rural community college students become engaged, recognizes the power of their experiences and voices, and makes visible a space for them in the academic world. At a time when a split between urban and rural is at the center of so many discussions, this approach to teaching American literature also does something else. It may, at times, provide a way to seeing all people's experiences as valuable. The academic world is lesser if rural students do not bring their particular perspectives to it. The academic world benefits from learning that this rural perspective is multifaceted and fascinating, certainly not monolithic.

This book hopes to bridge that cultural gulf, in some small way, so that the complexities of rural experiences may be welcomed and sought after in the community college classroom. Perhaps, with the confidence built from these experiences, rural students will see their place in the larger academic world.

Centralia College, Central Campus, 23 October 2014.

Introduction

This book first developed from experiences and interactions with students in my American literature classes at Centralia College, a rural community college in Washington State. Located halfway between Seattle, Washington, and Portland, Oregon, Centralia is in a vast rural, often heavily forested, landscape. The photo above was taken on central campus in the afternoon, when most of the two-thousand-plus full-time enrolled students are either in lab, have gone back to a local high school, or are at work. The busiest hours of the day on campus are between 8:00

a.m. and 12:00 noon, and then again after 5:00 p.m. until about 9:00 p.m., when the night classes run. Even before the shift to remote instruction in March 2020 due to the pandemic, there were numerous students taking classes through online and hybrid modalities who accessed the campus resources, faculty, and staff through the internet. The campus is three blocks long by two blocks wide. Most students live and work "nearby," which in a rural area means within fifty miles. Because of the small size of our student population and our comprehensive mission—"Centralia College is committed to student success, academic excellence, and supporting our community in an inclusive and equitable learning environment" ("Centralia College Mission")—most of the faculty members at Centralia College teach in several related disciplines, although each has a specific area of specialization.

I teach literature, composition, and humanities courses, and I began to notice a surprising pattern in all my classes but most obviously in my American literature survey course. When examining texts that are set in rural locations or have overtly rural characters, students whom I initially defined as "rural" were nearly invisible in class discussions. I expected their rural backgrounds to have added complications and layers of meaning, had those students chosen to highlight that knowledge. Instead, they "blended" into the rest of the class, choosing to remain silent. Rarely, a student who was well known as part of a rural community—for example, a student who was the county dairy princess or whose family held significant land and was already "known" for ties to agriculture—would proclaim this information but only in private writing to me. Generally, students were hesitant to show their expertise on rural issues. Even the composition student who was writing a research paper about the use of supplements in cattle raising would only share her work with the class if I asked her directly. What I would come to understand through this project was that my own image of a rural student was biased. I had internalized a rural student definition that assumed that all rural students are exclusively agriculturally based, with the student serving as a representative of a relatively homogenous culture. My definition was wrong. And because I was working from a set of incorrect assumptions, my concerns for students who seemed to be marginalized in my classroom did not result in changes to the ways students interacted in class discussions or in their written assignments.

When working and talking outside of class, in my office, or in the writing center, students would identify themselves as "rural," at least according to my initial narrow definition of a rural student. I had defined a rural student as a person who had direct experience with farming or ranching. They would reveal themselves, however, only when they saw and heard me refer to my experiences growing up in rural Iowa first. It was almost a secret to be shared with another "rural-identified" person who was hiding out in the academic world. They did not want their rural backgrounds to make their classmates think less of them or to think that the rural students did not belong in an academic environment. I was surprised that students who were engaged in agriculture directly, or who had strong family connections with farm or ranch life, were so hesitant to share their experiences in the classroom. I was so blinded by my own stereotyped definition of rural students that I assumed rural students would be *more* likely to share on a rural campus, not less. I assumed that nearly all the students had some degree of rural background, some portion of their identity tied to the local Centralia community, a small town in the middle of agricultural lands, national forests, and logging companies. I was surprised that these students expressed their feelings of being outsiders, people who did not really see themselves on a college campus nor think they had much to offer to the larger academic discussion. How could their knowledge of goats and land-use taxes be relevant to college conversations? My work to understand and ameliorate this problem led to this book. I hope to make a case for theorizing rural literacy and to develop critical pedagogical approaches for rural students in my community college and, by extension, for rural students in higher education, and to do so without reifying what it means to identify as rural.

This book is one attempt to address this disconnect between my expectations, some of my students' decisions not to participate fully in my American literature course, and my hope to improve the classroom experience, to better support my students in improving their skills, knowledge, and connection to the academic world. First, I needed to alter my misconceptions of rural students.

I came to understand that the term "rural students" is problematic at best but can be useful if I adjust my understanding rather than reinforcing a stereotype. For the purpose of this book, all students who are attending a rural community college are rural. They may have life experiences that reflect farming, or ranching, or logging, but not all do. What they all do have in common is that they currently live and attend college in a rural community, where distances between people and services may be significant. The digital divide is prominent, for example, with limited availability of Wi-Fi and high-speed internet. They also have direct and current experiences that call into question the ways that the rural is represented in the American literature texts we study in class.

As I will develop further later, the work of Kim Donehower, Charlotte Hogg, and Eileen Schell points out that there are culturally embedded representations of rural places and people that assert that the rural is missing aspects of urban life, or is lagging behind the times, or is an idealized location that projects a fictionally happy past (*Rural Literacies* 1). Rural students often have internalized the dominant culture's impressions, and despite my attempts to use Paulo Freire's critical pedagogy, I was not as successful as I'd hoped in providing an American literature classroom space that encouraged and supported rural students in developing their analyses of texts and language. By making a case for theorizing rural literacy and developing critical pedagogical approaches for rural students in higher education, I hope to engage rural students in richer, more significant explorations of American literature.

Prominent Concerns

I address several prominent concerns in this book. First, I needed to find a way to conceptualize a pedagogy that students could use to bring their experiences and expertise to the study of language. Second, although I was using critical pedagogy in my classes, it was not operating as successfully as I had expected with my student population, so I had to identify what was not working and reconceive a critical pedagogy in my classroom that would better connect my students' lives with the course content. Third, I had to clarify and resolve my own misconceptions and perceptions as I approached defining rural students. Finally, it was important to me that this work be of service to others in the field. Although I approached these concerns with my own students, this context is replicable. Professors working in small, rural community colleges can use the theoretical insights I share and build on the practical applications of these theories in their classrooms. As I approached these four key concerns, my first turn when looking for a way to restructure my pedagogical organization was to composition scholars. Because of the small size of my institution, everyone in the English department teaches primarily composition courses and then additional specialties, which for me includes American literature. Working across fields has brought me into contact with composition scholars' student-centered emphasis, and I have often found the ways that compositionists approach language to be useful in the literature classroom.

Some compositionists pay particular attention to critical pedagogies, ways of being in the classroom that explicitly triangulate the confluence of language, power, and place. Paula Mathieu's *Tactics of Hope: The Public Turn in English Composition* (2005), David Fleming's *City of Rhetoric: Revitalizing the Public Sphere in Metropolitan America* (2008), and Bruce McComiskey and Cynthia Ryan's edited collection, *City Comp: Identities, Spaces, Practices* (2003) all explore the gaps between what urban students bring to higher education and the expectations for their use of language in this new space. The challenges faced by urban students who bring a set of particular perspectives, experiences, and linguistic structures to the university setting has been a rich area of study, highlighting the tensions that emerge when the public space of higher education, with a formal set of conventions for writing, comes into contact with differences in social discourse. However, composition studies has paid less attention to the rural as a location from which students bring a knowledge set that may not translate easily and obviously into their experiences as critical scholars in higher education.

This book addresses that gap, with a special focus on rural students in university-level American literature courses. I turn to composition theory and practice because both the structures of critical pedagogy and the role that writing and rhetorical skills can play in literature courses are directly useful. I have built on these ideas of the interrelationship of power, place, and language to promote a critical literacy that embraces the experiences and knowledges of rural students. While I draw on my own campus and literature classroom as a case study in my book, the ramifications of this disconnect between how rural students conceptualize and share their expertise when problematizing rural representations apply to anyone who shares my concerns. This book expands the scholarly conversation for those who are working with similar students and within similar learning communities, as well as for those who seek to empower students from rural places in the classroom or in the world of higher education writ large.

Composition theories and pedagogy are useful critical thinking in my American literature class, and I see a space through which to approach my concerns about students not fully engaging all of their resources when deconstructing and analyzing literature. I want students to both participate more fully and to take a great degree of ownership in and connection to their studies. For me, empowering students means that they see themselves as legitimate participants in academic conversations. Empowered students understand that their experiences have value and that their contributions to class discussions enhance the discussions and activities. They recognize that they "belong" in higher education and engage with it. It is my hope to encourage them to connect their lived experiences with the classroom experiences while examining American literature texts. For my rural students, when those literary works include explicit representations of the rural and the people living in that space, thoughtful critiques of these texts are potentially fertile locations for more in-depth exploration.

One notable exception to compositionists' minimal focus on rural students is Kim Donehower, Charlotte Hogg, and Eileen E. Schell's book *Rural Literacies* (2007), which argues that individuals writing about the rural have built a version of the rural that suits their own needs and biases. Along with Donehower, Hogg, and Schell's later edited collection *Reclaiming the Rural: Essays on Literacy, Rhetoric, and Pedagogy* (2012), this text offers perspectives on literacy, rhetoric, and pedagogy in rural communities. My book adds to this conversation by using compositionists' concerns with hierarchy, hegemony, and language to equip students who come to higher education from rural spaces with rhetorical structures that enable them to push back against representations of the rural they encounter in introductory American literature courses. By building on their written rhetorical skills, I assert, when grappling with American literature texts, rural students will recognize the problematic and contradictory depiction of the geography, cultures, and people they know well.

In *Rural Literacies*, Donehower, Hogg, and Schell call for a closer examination of the traditional misrepresentation of rural places as locations for only "lack, lag, and the rosy past" (1). These misrepresentations assert that the rural is missing important economic or cultural attributes, is slow to follow the improvements of urbanized neighbors, or is the site of sweet memories of a fictional farm life where daily tasks are easy and simple and build moral character. I examined how these concepts play out in introductory American literature courses when framed as topoi, or rhetorical commonplaces, keywords and ideological formations that circulate in a social space. Topoi are commonly understood beliefs and understandings that provide a starting point for more complicated analysis. Through the tracing of and strategic use of these topoi, students may begin to understand how the images and representations in a work of literature do not reflect an absolute reality, but instead create merely one author's vision of rural places, which may or may not have clear connections with rural life.

As ubiquitous commonplaces, these three topoi of rural places provide a jumping-off point for students as they interrogate the extent to which rural spaces are or are not represented as places that lack cultural and economic resources available in urban spaces, as places that are behind in their cultural and economic development, or as places that represent an idealized, and perhaps fictionalized, past for urbanites (Donehower et al., *Rural* 1). My book uses these topoi as a framework from which a pedagogy that is critical in its stance calls all students to examine how representations of the rural may be revealed, obscured, altered, and created. Because topoi are commonly understood in the larger culture, they serve well as a beginning point for rural students to contest, challenge, resist, and orient themselves within the depictions of the rural that appear in American literature texts and public discourse more generally. They provide both the context and the structure for students to work from an uncritical acceptance of what appears in a work of literature to a more nuanced and complicated understanding of what that representation might achieve, what it might hide or minimize, and how literature is constructed by the author.

Donehower, Hogg, and Schell's contention of "lack, lag, and rosy past" is strongly evident in the work of previous scholars, as well as in United States government publications that focus on the rural. Repeatedly, those who do not live and work in rural areas use a particular construction of rural life in order to further their own agendas. Urban dwellers may scapegoat or oversimplify the rural to create an illusion of the superiority of cities, politicians may use a rural-versus-urban dichotomy to influence policy development, and those who have left a rural environment for an urban one may want to depict their choice as liberation from a diminished location and lifestyle. This clear connection supports my use of lack, lag, and rosy past as topoi, as these ideas are clearly in circulation.

Other scholars set the context and the prior conversation on repeated and familiar representations from which I have built a pedagogy that makes use of students' awareness, critique, and strategic deployment of these topoi. These conversations include Henry Nash Smith's mapping of shifts in imagery surrounding "domesticated" rural spaces; Leo Marx's work on what it means to be an American and how these areas may be considered in relation to other, quickly urbanizing areas; and Allen Batteau's statement that "Appalachia is a creature of the urban imagination" (1), which constructs a rural space that needs to be "filled" with the superior economic wisdom and culture of the urban. Further, I explored Mary Louis Pratt's conception of the "contact zone" (5–9) to discuss the rural as a contested space constructed though language. Pratt's ideas are useful to illustrate how students who have lived in these rural contact zones may engage in "autoethnographic expression" to "talk back" to the dominating powers outside of their communities (9). Talking back is critically important to me because, in this book, I explore how students from rural spaces can use their expertise with the rural to develop their own critical thinking skills, as well as to add to the richness of ideas present in their college classrooms.

This book adds to the conversation by considering what it means to develop critical pedagogies and envision critical public work within dominantly rural or small-town locations. Understanding rural literacies and developing pedagogy out of an understanding of students' prior literacy practices and rhetorical skills can help to connect rural undergraduates to their rightful place as engaged voices in the academy. A critical rural pedagogy can then be leveraged to enhance pedagogy in undergraduate American literature courses. My overall goal is to develop a practical embodiment of this theoretical call.

Purpose and Scope

As I mentioned above, rural topoi such as lack, lag, and rosy past may become points of argument from which students can discover how the language around these concepts controls, focuses, or defines experiences. Part of the aim of my proposed critical rural pedagogy is to ask students to engage in the historical genealogies/sources/legacies of these core topoi and how the topoi appear in literature. Because American literature offers an excellent vehicle for exploring the circulation of these topoi historically, I also briefly explore the extent to which these representations of the rural are included without critical interrogation in texts and ancillary materials students encounter in standard college literature readers. As part of my proposed critical rural pedagogy, students in rural places may read within and against these topoi and are well positioned to do so in interesting ways. Literature courses can also expand their critical discussions to ask students to pointedly locate themselves, their experiences, and their surroundings within the rhetorical structures and topoi they are reading that pertain to the rural. When instructors do not have firsthand knowledge of the rural, students from rural backgrounds can encourage, question, and develop contestations of the texts.

The use of the three topoi provides lenses for exploring everyday life for these students, an aim of a more critical pedagogy.

This book explores three main questions. 1) How can rural literacies be used strategically to enrich the teaching of American literature texts, especially when the term *rural literacy* is already highly contested? 2) How does the current theoretical structure, based in the topoi of lack, lag, and rosy past deployed in literature, complicate the ways students define rural peoples and places and their relationships to other Americans? 3) How might I develop a critical pedagogy, using composition theories of language, power, and place, that helps to build on and enhance students' rhetorical skills for deployment in the interrogation of and intervention in these texts in a rural classroom setting, and empower these students to use their expertise in rural life as a critical focus when examining texts?

In answering these driving questions, I also learned there are concerns that had to be included in my theorizing and application of theory. I will discuss them in greater detail in the chapters that follow, but I will summarize several of these points here. The term *rural* is contentious and defined by multiple governmental and educational entities to serve an often urban organizational and economic structure. Also, lack, lag, and rosy past have purchase throughout the dominant culture. These three topoi are stable points for contention; they appear in texts, and their use reflects deliberate strategies or culturally embedded attitudes. Students can explore how these terms are controlled, deployed, or perhaps resisted.

The concept of what constitutes rural literacies, as well as how and why one might go about promoting such literacies, is also contested. Students from rural areas bring a variety of literacies with them to the college classroom. Since the dominant discussion about rural pedagogy occurs at the K–12 level, those pedagogical techniques, strategies, or theories that use students' locally lived experiences as the basis for building knowledge and skills may inform working with rural students at the college level as well. An awareness of previously encountered rural pedagogies should better prepare professors for using the students' expertise as a basis for critical interrogation of representations of the rural.

Critical Pedagogy in Rural Community Colleges

Critical pedagogy is important to me because I work with community college students, a group who are often portrayed as less successful in the world of higher education. The American Association of Community Colleges' *Fast Facts 2022* points out that 65 percent of students attend part-time. Additionally, 40 percent of the students attending are taking noncredit courses. Despite the lower tuition and fees at community colleges, $3,800 annually versus $10,740 at public in-state four-year colleges, AACC also reports 56 percent of students are receiving financial aid. Additionally, most students, 62 percent of full-time and 72 percent of part-time, work while attending classes. I was not surprised to see that of those working, 21 percent of full-time students are also working full-time, with the rate of concurrent full-time work jumping to 38 percent for part-time students (*Fast Facts 2022*). According to the 2005 *TYCA Two-Year College Facts and Data Report*, partly funded by a 2004 CCCC Research Initiative grant, in the 1999–2000 academic year, "89 percent of all two-year college students are defined as . . . nontraditional, compared with 58 percent of public four-year students" (5–6). These statistics suggest a general marginalization of community college students (perhaps exaggerated within rural contexts) and the challenge of successful integration of these students into the world of higher education. Additionally, Centralia College is officially designated a public, rural-serving, medium-sized institution for federal Stafford loans. According to the college's accreditation report in 2011–2012:

> The college has a current enrollment of approximately 2,600 full time equivalent state supported students (FTEs) who are taught by an average of 117 full time equivalent faculty (FTEs) . . . . Centralia College is the nexus of higher education in District 12, Lewis and south Thurston counties, offering opportunities for higher education to the citizens of an essentially rural service district. Within this 2,400-square-mile district, numerous communities combine for a total population of approximately 75,000 people. The city of Centralia, where the college is located, is the most populous city in the district with a population of about 15,000 people. . . . Like many

> rural communities, the college's district has seen substantial changes in its workforce and economy. Lewis County has struggled with its shift from an agricultural, timber, and mining based economy to a service based economy. The Lewis County unemployment rate was 14.6 percent in February 2011, the highest in the state. (3)

Rural students at my community college are clearly working against and through stressors that may impede their success in higher education and in my literature classes, more specifically. I looked to the work of Freire in critical pedagogy precisely because he calls for the empowerment of students who are marginalized in some way. I wanted to use his theoretical work to provide my students with experiences and skills that allow them to push back against a hegemonic structure that places them in a position of powerlessness, voicelessness. I had hoped by using critical pedagogy my students would learn to speak back to power.

Why critical pedagogy? As Joe L. Kincheloe explains, "critical pedagogy works to help teacher educators and teachers reconstruct their work so it facilitates the empowerment of all students" (*Knowledge* 9), and I hoped this move also helps rural students attach to the university as a community where they belong and are valued. Aspects of critical pedagogy that are especially important for my students and this project include the facts that critical pedagogy is

- [g]rounded on a social and educational vision of justice and equality . . .
- [c]oncerned that schools don't hurt students—good schools don't blame students for their failures or strip students of the knowledges they bring to the classroom . . .
- [c]oncerned with "the margins" of society, the experiences and needs of individuals faced with oppression and subjugation . . . [and]
- [a]ttuned to the importance of complexity—understands complexity theory—in constructing a rigorous and transformative education. (10)

Kincheloe points out that working through texts using multiple or changing lenses is important because

> "[i]diosyncratic readings protect students from 'correct' interpretation and fixed meanings, as they, in the process, gain practice in recognizing the ways dominant power is attempting to shape their consciousness. . . . This is why critical teachers will study the same texts in different ways in different classes or in different semesters" (31).

While Kincheloe is talking about K–12 classrooms here, I had the same goal for my students at the community college. And despite the complications of working with students who occupy positions of marginalization and positions of power, sometimes concurrently, as I discuss more deeply in Chapter 2, by using a reformation of critical pedagogy, a critical rural pedagogy, it is possible to harness the transformative power of multiple perspectives when working through an American literary text and having students create rhetorical responses to that text.

On the Rural

As part of the need to clarify and resolve misperceptions, I interrogate the concepts of the "rural" and "rural literacy" in much greater detail in Chapter 2. To introduce these ideas, here I establish a baseline from which to work. Let me begin by clarifying the term "rural." Doing so is critical because definitions of the "rural" are problematic. The concerns that underlie this book are revealed when examining who defines the rural, for what purposes the rural is defined, and how rural geographic space is delimited. In defining the "rural," I seek to avoid reinforcing perceptions that minimize or perpetuate stereotypes of rural peoples and experiences; rather, my understanding of the rural seeks to illustrate the complex lives of people who live in the American rural.

There is not a singular rural experience or homogenous population. Instead, rural students bring with them varieties of home cultures and language, unique sets of experiences currently in the rural space. The rural is not a static location. Instead, the rural encompasses ranges. For example, some people in rural spaces remain in one location for long periods of their lives, but there are others who move in and out of rural spaces and for varying amounts of time. To generalize them as having the same understandings of the world, and to further diminish rural peoples by suggesting they are not aware of or in touch with the rest of the world, is incorrect.

Defining the rural, or defining any geographical space/landscape, has long proven problematic. Krista Comer, who theorizes the intersection between gender and geography in the American West, asserts that "landscape is not an empty field of vision (the premise of perceptual geography) but rather a brimming-full social topography that creates and enacts the various cultural assumptions and power struggles of the age" (13). Building on her statement, the mechanisms and imagery through which the rural is identified or seen in context against other landscapes/spaces highlights "cultural assumptions and power struggles" (13). A definition of the rural then must and should illuminate, and engage in, these struggles.

Despite Comer's call, there are multiple definitions highlighting what the rural is not rather than what it is. A consistent definition would seem important for the many government agencies that regulate and monitor activities in the rural, but even those agencies operate with different definitions. For example, the United States Department of Agriculture (USDA) points to the problem of defining the rural in their updated publication "What Is Rural?": "many people have definitions for the term rural, but seldom are these rural definitions in agreement" (Reynnells and John). While I agree that there are multiple definitions, I disagree with their solution, which is to define the urban/suburban based on population density, and then to call anything that drops below a certain number rural. The second federal agency I consulted, the General Accounting Office, identifies areas designated metro/urban, and "nonmetro/rural is then defined by exclusion—any area that is not metro/urban is nonmetro/rural" (Reynnells and John). The urban is the space to be highlighted, and then whatever is left out must be rural. A third government agency, the Bureau of the Census, defines urbanized areas by population, specifically as having "a population of 50,000 or more and a population density generally exceeding 1,000 people per square mile . . . all urbanized areas with a population of 2,500 or more that are not adjacent to identified urban areas are also considered urban population.

All others are considered rural" (Reynnells and John). There is no call to define the rural on its own, or to define the rural first so that what is left is urban or suburban.

A fourth governmental entity, the Office of Management and Budget, uses the Bureau of the Census definitions to carve out "metropolitan statistical areas [MSAs]," and "any county not included in an MSA is considered nonmetro" (Reynnells and John). The name suggests a hierarchical structure with the urban holding greater value and importance, so much so that anything outside this classification is a "non" or not important / not normative / not valuable / not worth spending the time and effort to isolate on its own. Each of these four agencies defines the rural, an "othered" classification—as what is left over, what is outside of the organizing system. Additionally, these classification systems suggest that all rural areas are perceived flatly, patently identical in their great lack of the urban.

Surprisingly, even the USDA picks up terminology that foregrounds what is missing in rural areas, using a sliding scale that designates 0–3 metro, whereas areas that score 4–9 are "nonmetro . . . [until] 9 = completely rural or urban population of fewer than 2,500, not adjacent to a metro area" (Reynnells and John). Strikingly, within their definition, the USDA refers to an "urban population," which supposedly does not exist in the rural. And then to be the most rural, if there is a gathering of 2,500 people, they must also be at a distance from, or at least not right next to, an urban area. The rural is defined by default, lack, and separation from the urban.

Given this repeated use of the urban to define the rural, I offer the following definition of the rural, which does not reinforce a hierarchy with the rural at the bottom or as a space that is empty of people, power, or cultural value. When I use the term "rural," therefore, I purposely reflect an expansive definition that seeks to honor the multiplicity of peoples, cultural structures and contributions, and relevancy of the spaces called rural.

Rural areas are geographical spaces where inhabitants have developed a variety of connections that work with and around significant physical distance, either between residences or between individuals who work and interact with one another as a community. Accounting for much greater distances makes rural spaces substantially different from urban spaces. This greater distance influences how people interact, what resources are or are not available, how property is used and valued, and the circumstances under which social bonds are built and maintained. Rural areas are constantly under change due to shifts in the global market and the need to communicate effectively over distance. This pressure of constant adjustment requires flexibility in worldview, economic base, and interactions with those outside of each rural area. Each rural location has unique dominant challenges related to geography, immigration patterns, etc.

In keeping with this clearer understanding, I widened my own definition of rural students. For this book, I assert that all the students who attend classes through my campus are rural. The rural includes tremendous diversity, and my students are reflective of this. They include people of a wide range of ages—from fourteen or fifteen up through mid-sixties—people who come from multiple ethnic groups, people who speak English often, but just as often have a home language or two that is not English, and people who are from a range of economic classes, social identities, abledness, ethnicities, and gender identities. My students experience various degrees of success as they transfer on to larger four-year universities to complete degrees or as they move on to work in the wider community after completing associate's degrees.

On Rural Literacy

There is tremendous contention around the term *rural literacy*, and my book clarifies the existence of that contention in current knowledge and practice. The use of the term is important in this book because knowing what literacies have been emphasized for students who are now attending a rural community college provides a starting point, and a common set of skills and abilities, a baseline for building a critical rural pedagogy. However, the scholars I consulted developed their definitions from disparate perspectives, leading to a multitude of literacies loosely collected under the umbrella term *rural literacy*. I explore this conundrum more fully in Chapter 2, but I present a brief overview here to illustrate the range of meanings of this term, as it is currently being used. To cite just a few of these scholars, rural literacy has been defined as "literate skills needed to achieve the goals of sustaining life in rural areas" (Donehower et al., *Rural Literacies* 4); or as a way to "read" rural spaces and peoples (Edmondson 63–66); or as missing memorization skills in elementary school children (Petrosky 65); or as an expertise in using resources available to rural peoples (Hautecoeur 9–19); or finally, as the ways women in Appalachia maintain their nonacademic dialect when writing in academic situations (Sohn 5). The range of their definitions of rural literacy was surprising.

I did not discover a consensus in content, structure, purpose, or object for the term *rural literacy*. However, it is clear that rural literacy has multiple threads that a critical rural pedagogy needs to consider and attend to. Rural literacy is tied to a particular geographical location, in which an individual needs to successfully operate linguistically. Next, rural literacy includes the ability to use reading and writing to form identity and place within a rural community and discourses that circulate within that community. Finally, rural literacy may be a vision of what students should know or be able to perform, based on the needs of outsiders who want to control the rural for their own purposes. This definition may serve as the basis for resistance, and for a critical pedagogy that will allow students to enact a richer response to texts. My proposed critical rural pedagogy considers these varying threads and determines how to use them to empower rural students in college American literature classes to participate in critical conversations that have meaning for them. It is my hope that this will help them recognize the importance of their presence in and contribution to higher education not only in my classes but in similar settings.

Critical Pedagogy and the Rural

Because critical pedagogy is important to both empower students and engage them in classroom interactions, in this book I have theorized a variation of critical pedagogy that is more likely to engage rural students. I have called this variation *critical rural pedagogy*. In order to build this variation, I first explored the forms of pedagogy that have been advocated for use with rural students, and I have anticipated constructing a form that would connect with useful pedagogies that rural students may have encountered in their previous years of formal schooling. However, just as rural literacies turned out to be a slippery term in practice, so too are the pedagogies used in rural settings.

There are numerous pedagogical discussions that do not connect seamlessly with each other, and most of the discussion is focused on students in grades K–12. Pedagogical conversations tend to focus on curriculum rather than on teaching strategies. The discussion of pedagogy that specifically targets rural students also tends to homogenize students into a single cultural or ethnic group, and this works against the diversity of students I encounter in my rural community college classroom. Despite these concerns, it was vital to determine whether there is a rural pedagogy, and if not, to determine how the pedagogical concerns of teachers and instructors might illustrate concerns I need to consider when creating a critical rural pedagogy.

An overview of the current pedagogical discussions around rural students and rural issues illustrates the ways pedagogy may be an attempt to control the rural, or to create a vision of the rural that creates a particular set of values that may or may not be connected to the current local rural culture. While a more complete discussion of these pedagogical calls appears in Chapter 2, what follows is a distillation to illustrate the perspectives presented by scholars of rural pedagogies. David Orr calls for a "re-ruralization," or a curriculum that assumes rural people do not move from a specific location (231). Meanwhile, Toni Haas and Paul Nachtigal envision a special rural "lifeway" that gives priority to "deeper bonds with family, friends, and the world around them" (vi) rather than material gain. In a separate text, Nachtigal calls for the elimination of consolidated schools and a return to smaller numbers of students per school so that local context can be highlighted rather than following statewide curricular mandates ("Theme V" 309). Interestingly, one of the few pedagogical pieces to focus on rural students in higher education calls out how misunderstanding is not only possible, but likely, when professors are often "cosmopoles [. . .] a class of transient exotics" (Zencey 16), who are not in a position to understand the value of connection to a specific place because they themselves have moved away from their places of origin.

In short, this book makes clear the wide-ranging use of the term *rural pedagogy*. And, specifically, this project takes a critical tone in examining the ways rural pedagogy is used as a "stand-in" for curricular choices and the consequences of controlling terms for students in rural contexts.

Toward a Critical Rural Pedagogy

Given a definition of the rural as constituted of diverse people, practices, cultures, and geographies, this book offers a concept of *critical rural pedagogy* that is responsive to this diversity and to the aims of critical pedagogy. In developing and theorizing critical rural pedagogy, I put forth the following key characteristics of such pedagogy.

First, acceptance and problematizing of students' use of language based in rural experience is required. Rural students bring dynamic, situated vocabulary and language patterns that are not generally acknowledged in a higher education setting. For example, terms to denote specific ages, genders, and uses of livestock befuddle those who live in urban spaces. This complicated, rich understanding of animal husbandry is often mysterious to professors and classmates who have not lived in rural areas. As another example, the distances rural students travel for everyday activities, often driving miles between grocery stores, religious services, school, and work, has a powerful effect on how students see themselves in the geographic space of the rural. Going "over" to visit a friend has both a social and a time element embedded in the language choices students make to articulate this multilayered concept. Freire's thoughts on the teacher-student relationship, along with his criticisms of education as a bank rather than as transformative experience (72), provide a way to approach this gap. Creating a classroom dynamic where students are elevated from the oppressed to a position of some partnership in their learning, according to Freire, should enhance their learning experiences, and would encourage them to share their rural knowledge and insights.

David Bartholomae is a composition theorist who provides deeper insights on the distinction between academic language and the language practices that students bring with them. He laid important groundwork when he pointed out the difficulties students entering higher education face in learning academic discourse. The problem of "power and finesse," according to Bartholomae, lies in students' awareness of audience (595). From my experience, students from rural locations generally have an awareness of the assumptions about rural and urban that are carried in the university environment. They are cautious about bringing their previous experiences into play in a college classroom, where urbanized space is constantly assumed to be "normal," making the rural students' background, by comparison, abnormal. Urban-focused academic language does not include Carhartts, cattle squeezes, or distance as a factor in getting to stores, schools, and friends. Instead, a critical rural pedagogy creates curricular ways to include students' rural experiences, makes links between their experiences and the representations of the rural in literature, and develops critical thinking skills as they push within and against rural topoi they encounter in literature and their everyday lives.

Second, giving students an opportunity to develop tactics and skills for building writing skills and critical thinking is necessary. Activities, classroom discussion, written assignments, projects, and creative output in a critical rural pedagogy require instructors to design assignments that "provide the opportunity for engagement and growth" (Tinberg and Nadeau 116). Michel de Certeau's construction of strategies versus tactics is informative, providing possibilities for rural students to operate against the strategies of the larger educational structure (34–39). He points out that "strategies" are official rules and practices of government and cultural institutions (thus, are transparent, unchanging, rigid, etc.), so capturing the fluid moments of a more tactical response allows rural students, who may be described as marginalized, to enact a powerful reaction to their situation in college classrooms. This book explores how and when rural students can use their prior knowledge to push back against simplistic understandings of the complicated, messy, and at times error-filled representations that appear in specific works of American literature and broader public discourses. For example, when Emerson waxes poetic about cattle lying down as peaceful symbols, rural students need a strategy that helps them share what is basic knowledge for a rural child: a "down" cow is a sick cow, a serious situation for the animal and for those who are hoping to sustain a living by raising cattle. As a second example, when James Russell Lowell ties the imagery of rural fields and his idyllic childhood to a flower in his poem "To the Dandelion," rural students can bring a more complex understanding of the landscape Lowell describes.

Third, a rural critical pedagogy would need to contextualize rural students who occupy multiple hegemonic positions, as they may align themselves with dominant American culture, and at the same time be marginalized and othered. The persistent and dominant representations of the rural, which foreground what is missing, what is lagging behind, or what is connected with a fictionalized, mythic past, are forced upon rural students by government agencies, urban curriculum developers, and others. However, creating pedagogically sound activities and writing assignments that embrace the multiple positions of these students is imperative for exploring the richness of the texts and students' positions in relation to them. The feminist pedagogical movement has significant insights into working with marginalized topics and peoples to offer here, especially when there are issues of power hierarchies and enshrined cultural attitudes. As one example, Melanie Kaye/Kantrowitz writes specifically about "teaching across difference" by using multiple lenses in the classroom to destabilize dominate theories, cultural constructs, and individual biases (281). She models ways for rural students to express more problematized interpretations of representations of the rural in texts and in their written analysis of such texts. Example activities in Chapter 3 build on feminist approaches.

Chapter Overview

Chapter 1 addresses the concern that students in my rural community college American literature classes often do not engage their experiences and knowledge about the rural when the studied texts provide a flat, one-dimensional, or awkward construction of rural places and people. It is important to have students who not only are willing to complicate their understanding of these texts but bring their perspectives as rural students into the classroom. I next identify common patterns of representations of the rural in American texts: as locations that lack substantial aspects of urban/suburban life, as locations that lag behind, or as locations that represent a rosy past. Those culturally embedded, commonly reproduced patterns are then not only appropriate, but also ideally suited, topoi for structuring the tensions that exist around rural representations in texts and ways students might argue back to, or complicate, these representations.

Chapter 2 explores how rural literacies currently in the culture are or, more frequently, are not employed in current pedagogy used with rural students. I also examine rural pedagogy, a contended term, and how it has been used by teachers, policymakers, and scholars. Much to my surprise, my search for rural literacies and how they are enacted in rural pedagogy revealed that despite the rich and productive use of varieties of literate skills and situations in rural areas, current pedagogy makes scant use of students' literacies, either as a baseline to work from or as a set of skills and knowledges students can enact in the classroom. Later in Chapter 2, I argue for a variation of critical pedagogy, which I call critical rural pedagogy. I argue for a critical rural pedagogy and suggest aspects of that pedagogy that are central to working with rural students in rural settings. Just a few of these aspects, which I will discuss more fully in Chapter 2, include the claims that a critical rural pedagogy needs to encourage and support students when they use their previous rural language experiences, helps students develop tactics and skills to reveal the biases that limit representations of the rural, and recognizes the concurrent and multiple locations these students occupy within hegemonic structures of the dominant culture, economic class, and geographic location.

Chapter 3 completes this move to classroom application by using rural critical pedagogy, as outlined in Chapter 2, as a basis for classroom activities, assignments, and techniques. Due to space constraints, I limit this discussion to the works of four American literature authors, Robert Frost—Flannery O'Conner—Henry David Thoreau—Alice Walker, and the ways their works are contextualized in the ancillary materials found in anthologies. I am also interested in how anthology editors reflect the echoes of the three topoi—rural people and locations as places that are without cultural importance, places that are hopelessly behind urbanized locations, or places that are heavily mythologized spaces to be kept as idealized locations. I chose these four authors' works because they are commonly taught in introductory courses and because of their explicit focus on rural locations and peoples. I end the chapter with specific examples of activities and assignments to use when exploring these same four authors' works to enact a critical rural pedagogy. These activities serve both to illustrate the use of critical rural pedagogy and to create a starting point that other scholars and professors of American literature may build upon.

Chapter 4 concludes with lessons learned from this project and makes suggestions about the next steps that I and others can take in further developing critical rural pedagogy.

In sum, this book seeks to directly address the ways that rural students are not empowered, not fully engaged by critical pedagogy, in my American literature survey course at Centralia College. Instead, I argue for the use of a variation of critical pedagogy that explicitly addresses the multiple positions of power and marginalization rural students occupy, and that enact the topoi of lack, lag, and rosy past as scaffolding that empowers rural students and develops structures for students to enter into conversation with these texts in ways that build on multiple perspectives on the rural. I share activities and written assignments to model critical rural pedagogy as it can appear in my classroom and to serve other American literature professors. It is my expectation that my peers in other rural community colleges will further build on these activities and engage in a continued conversation around the issues I have raised for American literature students.

Chapter One

Seen but Not Seen: Who Is Rural?

As described in my introduction, I explore representations of the rural in American literature texts and how these representations, created by authors for their own purposes, serve to distance rural students from the academic world. I believe these representations, when viewed through the lens of a critical pedagogy, and more specifically of a critical rural pedagogy might be leveraged to facilitate the academic empowerment of rural community college students enrolled in American literature introductory survey courses. I begin with a closer exploration of how and why critical pedagogy falls short as a theoretical and practical tool when used with my rural students. Then, I explore the ways the rural is represented by the dominant culture and how those ways can be leveraged as topoi, providing students a possible structure to work through when questioning and exploring those dominant representations in their American literature readings.

Dominant Rural Representations: Lack, Lag, and Rosy Past

Vignette: Challenges to Critical Pedagogy in a Rural Community College

It seemed a typical day in my American literature survey course at Centralia College, a community college with a little over two thousand full-time enrolled students, located in a rural community halfway between Seattle, Washington, and Portland, Oregon. Students arrived in class, unpacked their books and notes, and began discussing the day's reading,

Emerson's "To Each and All." This poem, first published in 1839, is an exploration of the persona's return to a rustic retreat, a rural hermitage, where he can become reconnected with a "perfect whole" (McMichael and Leonard 581). In assigning this text, it was my hope that students would become familiar with the work of a major American literary figure, continue to improve their practical skills in close reading of poetry, and finally, question the imagery of the poem, both in purpose and in impact. As dictated by the course outline, we were exploring texts that are generally recognized as part of a traditional literary canon. We began class, as usual, by working from questions students had developed about the reading before the class session.

Most of my students are not English majors. My campus offers only one American literature course, a general survey, which is taught once or perhaps twice each academic year. Students choose this course from a list of required options to fulfill a three-course humanities requirement for the associate of arts degree. For most of my students, this is the first and only college-level literature course they are likely to take. Because my community college is the primary access to higher education in the county, my students include traditional age first- and second-year students, but the age range expands decades beyond this narrow group. There are "running-start" students (dual-enrolled local high school students) who have chosen the course because it also meets their requirements for a high school literature course. Even younger students, often fifteen or sixteen years old, have come to the college after completing their homeschooling programs.

My oldest students are typically in their late fifties, returning to school after years away or attending for the first time. My classroom is also populated with veterans, working single parents, recent immigrants, and the occasional international student. Although the vast majority of students are white, a larger number of Latinx students are coming to campus each year. There are also international students from Asia, Africa, and the Middle East. Economically, some of the youngest students may come from privileged homes, and they are taking advantage of the running-start program to get ahead on their general requirements before heading to larger universities. However, most students at Centralia College are paying their own way, working part- or full-time jobs and managing family responsibilities. Their drive to improve their economic lot is central to their motivations for going to college. To generalize, my students pursue most of the majors and areas of emphasis offered across campus, ranging from physics to political science, music, and criminal justice. Quite a few students are also working toward completing a variety of transferable "upside-down" degrees, which allow students who wish to transfer into identified majors (such as welding, biology, early childhood, or business) to concentrate on their discipline-specific courses while at the community college. In other words, students are focused on their chosen area of study, which is most definitely not American literature.

For the students in class that day, parsing the meaning, structure, patterns of construction, and metaphors in the text before them was not at the top of their list of priorities. As first-year college students, they would be able to improve on whatever skills they brought with them for critical reading, textual analysis, and writing. I realize that generalizations are fraught with oversimplifications, but I have learned to expect several reactions to the course. A small number of students are avid readers. While not necessarily English majors, they have a powerful love of written texts and look forward to "digging in" to new works. I also know there will be students who have done quite a bit of close textual analysis through their religious affiliations, having parsed important wisdom literature over their lives, most often the Bible and the Book of Mormon. However, most of my students are somewhat bemused. They do not walk into the classroom expecting course content that will be directly applicable to their lives or future professions. American literature is yet another course that some distant authority figure determined is a required hoop through which they must jump to earn a degree. Common reactions include mild interest, boredom, and/or concern centered on earning a particular grade. If some students have enrolled in my section of American literature because it is the only class that "fits" their schedule requirement, I may be confronted with outright hostility.

In class that day, we worked our way through discussions about the construction of the poem, the line lengths, and the use of stanzas. We discussed whether rhyme was necessary to qualify this text as a "poem" in their understanding, as well as questions about pronunciation of words that seemed to be "not quite right" rhymes. Finally, we were about to dive into the more critical conversation about how the poem's construction created specific meanings, perhaps for a particular reason, by a particular author, to attain some specific cultural, political, or economic gain. Because class members have usually lived in rural places, I assumed they would willingly share insights that would break open that discussion on the differences they noticed between the ways the poem depicts the rural and their experience-based understanding of rural life in especially fruitful ways. I was wrong.

I thought that because some students were familiar with cattle, having grown up on or near farms, lines 3 and 4 of Emerson's poem, "The heifer that lows in the upland farm, / Far-heard, lows not thine ear to charm" would provide material that students could relate to and that could open a critical conversation. Persons who have worked with cows would see that Emerson's imagery is not a realistic portrayal. I thought students who grew up in rural settings might notice the disconnect between their experiences and the poem right away. I foolishly assumed they would leap to point out that a single heifer seemed odd, as well as the sound Emerson ascribes to the animal. Cattle do make a low, grumbly sound sometimes referred to as "lowing," and most obviously this term calls to mind hymns sung around the winter holiday season most students would be familiar with ("the cattle are lowing, the poor baby wakes; but little lord Jesus no crying he makes"). However, single heifers, cows that are older than one year but have not yet had a calf, are noticeably and dependably quiet unless there is another cow they are communicating with, there is food arriving in the form of additional hay or grain, or they are in some sort of distress. None of these instances fits the scene created in the poem—a solitary horseman is riding through the area, noting the peace.

Here, I thought, was a clear, easy way to identify the distinction between the constructed world of the poem and the real world it purports to illustrate that also draws on students' situated and cultural knowledge. Here, I thought, I have found a way for my students to connect the reading of literature to their everyday lives. This distinction would help students to draw on their personal experiences, based on my understanding of the goals that develop when using critical pedagogy. While an awareness of the distinction between the world shown in a poem and students' lives is not necessarily constituted as a negative, in a first-year literature course, noticing this distinction is an early and important step in helping students critically evaluate texts, not as mirrors of truth because they are in the textbook, but as rhetorical constructions that are created by an author for a specific purpose and in a specific cultural and historic context. Interrogating the difference between students' experiences of rural places and the constructed rural world they encounter in the poem provides a starting structure for a critical examination of the entire poem, including the historical context in which it was created and the agents who would gain from this created image of the rural world. Discussions of hegemony, political stratification, economic practicalities of publishing in the time of the poem's creation, and connections to dominant movements in poetic theory and cultural attitudes are all available for further exploration once students grasp the fact that each text is constructed for a purpose by a person or persons with a number of aims that may or may not align with readers' expectations.

I assumed that students from the local area would notice that Emerson's representation did not match their experiences and speak up. I assumed that their familiarity with life in a rural community and their already developed rural literacy would give them not only recognition of this gap but the language to speak back against Emerson's simplistic, and clearly fictional, imagery. However, my attempts to use prompts, hints, exercises in exegesis, imagery identification, and questions about the possible interpretations of the poem all led to similar dead ends. Students were unwilling to see the poem as anything but Emerson's "truth." Because his work is located in the textbook, they were unwilling to question the work's accuracy in the rural context.

I was concerned by this unexpected nonresponse initially but became more concerned when this same pattern was repeated when we read other selections from American literature that highlighted rural imagery that did not match rural life as my students had experienced it. When we read Thomas Jefferson's *Notes on the State of Virginia*, they were silent as Jefferson extolled the greater virtue of people who work the land, as "the chosen people of God, if ever he had a chosen people, whose breast he has made his peculiar deposit for substantial and genuine virtue . . . [who] keeps the sacred fire, which otherwise might escape from the face of the earth" (297). My repeated questions about whether people who farm are morally superior, in their experience, were avoided. Later in the term, students did not bring their expertise into classroom discussion when we parsed the description of the Van Tassel farm in Washington Irving's "The Legend of Sleepy Hollow," an impossibly productive and valuable homestead. My attempts to draw them into recognizing the dichotomy created by Nathaniel Hawthorne between the village and the forest in "Young Goodman Brown" were met with equal resistance. My students were steadfast in their reluctance to discuss the ways that Henry David Thoreau describes the cultivated countryside around Walden Pond. This self-silencing was especially odd because my classes tend to be quite talkative, with students eagerly bringing in references to popular culture, urban experiences, and the news of the day.

It is important for students to connect their college experiences with the larger world, and I had thought texts with rural imagery would allow students to take advantage of what I believed was an obvious connection. Along with the cultural value of shared texts that an American literature class can provide, there is value in using these texts to build students' skills and confidence in working with complicated written works. Encouraging students to become active participants in their learning, as well as helping them to see their concerns, ideas, and interpretations as valuable in the academic world, is an important goal. I thought that if I provided students with a way to push back against dominant representations through techniques developed out of critical pedagogy, they would be able to empower themselves and see their place in the academic world. My intentions may have been well placed, but clearly my understanding and execution of critical pedagogy were lacking.

It was my intention to use critical pedagogy to encourage students to interrogate texts at multiple levels, with a significant focus on the purposes of these texts for the author, for the readers, for the larger culture, and for students in the present time. It is my observation that students navigating the world of higher education can be well served both in my classes and beyond by developing an empowering critical stance. As explained by Henry Giroux, "critical pedagogy attempts to understand how power works through the production, distribution, and consumption of knowledge within particular institutional contexts and seeks to constitute students as particular subjects and social agents" (31). I want my students to see themselves as active participants in the larger social context that extends beyond the classroom. By exploring the power structures that underlie which representations of the rural are developed and repeated by the dominant culture, they may be able to shift from a passive, nearly silent position in the classroom to a more active position. Giroux's assertion that critical pedagogy helps students believe they have the ability and power to "shape [democracy's] outcomes" addresses exactly the concern I have for my self-silenced students (33).

However, I had stumbled on a concern that was not fully addressed by the theories within critical pedagogy. As succinctly summarized by Joe Kincheloe, "critical pedagogy is interested in the margins of society, the experiences and needs of individuals faced with oppression and marginalization" (*Critical* 23). My rural students in agricultural production, who may live and work on family farms, are certainly marginalized by dominant culture, as I will explore in much more detail later in this chapter, but there are profound ways in which they may not see themselves as members of an oppressed or marginal group. My students tend to align themselves with the dominant culture in the United States. They are nearly all white, their belief systems are most often Protestant, they describe themselves as middle class, and nearly all of them speak English as their primary, and often only, language. They are able to hide their knowledge of agriculture, farming, or ranching by altering what they are wearing and avoiding sharing their rural knowledge. I was thoughtlessly unaware that they would be subjected to stress when asked to reveal their expert knowledge of rural experiences, issues, and outlooks, or to identify with oppressed groups or perspectives. My students were not necessarily looking to be empowered, at least not in the way I was initially imagining their empowerment. Additionally, the students in my rural community college classroom include students from a wide variety of backgrounds, experiences, and ages. This further complicates my attempts to treat them as a homogenous group of marginalized students, making my use of critical pedagogy further problematic. My pedagogical aims hope to speak to this diversity and these tensions rather than smooth them out.

After the class discussion of Emerson's poem, I spoke with several of the students I know who raise cattle. They live on small farms and have participated in the county fairs, showing heifers, bulls, and calves. Each one expressed surprise that I expected them to bring their rural and agricultural expertise into class discussion. When I pressed my students, insisting that their rural experiences can be a valuable source of information for work in the classroom, they were universally reluctant. They did not want their classmates to know they were "country" people. They expressed concern that such a label would also suggest they were not as bright, or not as aware of the rest of the world, as their classmates. I was familiar with the stereotypes, but I was stunned that my students seemed to have internalized these ideas to such a significant degree that it silenced them. They assumed that classmates would cast them in a negative light, despite the fact that there were people in the class who knew full well that they lived on cattle farms and had shown livestock at agricultural fairs. What I did not realize at the time was that I was also reflecting a biased representation of rural peoples as based in agriculture and perhaps a long tradition of agricultural endeavors. I was painting myself into a corner, reinforcing the very stereotypes that limit these students' understanding of their voices, their importance in the academic world.

They expressed a vision of two distinct worlds, the world of college and the world of home. I was reminded of David Bartholomae's work on the need for students entering the university system to learn to use unfamiliar discourses that do not correspond to their previous language use, either in their homes or in K–12 academic experiences. He points out that "the student needs to learn to speak our language, to speak as we do" in multiple academic genres and discourses (589–90). I began to see a possible theoretical construct, a way to consider the ways students position themselves in separate physical and intellectual places that might help me address this disconnect among their multiple worlds. By understanding how similar gaps operate in the ways students do or do not see themselves belonging in higher education, I can formulate class activities so that students might be able to push back against their self-imposed silence and develop a willingness to voice their perspectives in questioning texts or the representations that minimized their participation in my class and in society. Later, in Chapter 2, in addition to Bartholomae, I will be following the concerns raised by scholars who explore the gap between students' previous experiences and the requirements of a college setting, including Eric Zencey and Valerie Mulholland. This theorized gap is illustrated by my rural community college students' reluctance to connect their already acquired rural knowledge with analysis in a college classroom of texts that have rural imagery.

Complications with Applying Critical Pedagogy

My training and time spent working in composition had certainly prepared me for students who do not see themselves as full members of the academic world, but I had not for a second considered the possibility that rural students might have an equally powerful sense that they do not belong in higher education, or that they would consider their experiences prior to and parallel with their college courses as useless in academic discussions. Certainly, I had never considered the possibility that these students did not want to be identified with their rural lives. My classes are populated with students from all sorts of backgrounds, but I had not considered the ease with which students whom I would classify as having "rural" experience would hide that background. I had considered students who have lived in rural areas, or who have worked on family farms, or for whom hunting and spending time in the outdoors is not just recreation but part of a culture, to be rural. They may not currently be living in a rural setting, but they have grown up with a different set of expectations for family, for their connection to community, and for how they see themselves in relation to specific geographic locations. They can easily "pass" for urban or suburban students when they wish. They can easily dress, speak, and act in ways that hide their rural knowledge for short periods of time, for example, a class period. However, I came to realize that students without agricultural backgrounds who attend my rural community college are also "rural." They are living and working in a rural space, and that geographic location provides them with a perspective that has significant distinctions from suburban or urban students. All rural students have an awareness of the richness and diversity in the rural. They understand the challenges and gifts of living and working in a place where distance is both significant and a driver of choices, for instance when there is no bus service, and a car or a friend's car is the only real transportation option. All my rural students' input and perspectives are important in the academic world.

I consider all the students who attend classes at Centralia College to be part of the complicated tapestry of the rural even though not all of them come from rural backgrounds. I realized early in the work for this book that my own understanding of rural students was flattened, not comprehensive. I was considering only those students who lived and worked on farms and ranches as "rural." This misconception on my part certainly did not help my students, and explains, in part, why my previous efforts to bring students into fuller conversation were fraught with disappointment and unfulfilled good intentions. Once I thought more deeply about this question, and looked at just who is enrolled in my classes, I realized that I needed to update my previously held ideas about rural students. Although my definition is also incomplete, at this point based on the students who attend my rural community college, I have developed a working definition. All my students are rural. They attend a rural community college, and they include individuals with a wide variety of backgrounds, interests, economic positions, cultural connections, and experiences. They occupy multiple positions of power, often at the same time. Many white students see themselves clearly aligned with the dominant culture, but they are also, in some ways overtly and others more subtly, othered or marginalized because of the place they live, work, and attend college. In the same classroom, students of color, and students from historically marginalized populations, may see themselves as additionally marginalized due to where they live and work. Students on a rural campus are also different from students at suburban and urban college campuses because they can call on their perspective as persons who are in the rural when confronting representations of the rural. Their daily interactions in a rural space give them a chance to use an awareness heightened by their everyday lives.

Each student is a unique configuration of these shifting and parallel alliances and identities. One example is Alexis. She first came to Centralia College after graduating from her local high school, W. F. West in Chehalis, Washington. The high school serves 950 students in grades 9 through 12 ("W. F. West"). Alexis lived outside of town, actually physically closer to the smaller Napavine School District, which only serves around 750 students in grades kindergarten through 12 ("About Our District"), so she would drive ten miles each day in to the larger town's high school. She enrolled at Centralia College to complete an associate of arts degree with an intent to transfer on to a university after two years. She lived with her parents and brother on a small acreage outside of town limits. She began classes with some awareness of her white privilege but also a keen sense of economic divisions. She needed to pay for her classes, so accessing financial aid, working while going to school, and living at home were included in her strategy. Raising rabbits was her passion, and she had advanced from simply raising rabbits to judging rabbits at the local and state fair levels. She traveled across the state extensively and developed a large network within the bunny world. She had also traveled to Italy on a trip sponsored by her high school that included recent graduates and community members. Initially unsure of her major, Alexis began to take the standard core courses for an AA, and she focused her electives on courses in creative writing and English. She began to work in the writing center. Each student in my rural community college brings similarly complicated and interesting lives with them into the classroom. Because these students occupy a rural space, they are in a position to contest representations of the rural that are not equally complicated and multilayered.

I needed to find a way to bring rural students into discussions and activities in my American literature classes so that they would both add to the complexity of the entire class's deconstructions of texts and empower rural students. One possible solution is to bring rural students' knowledge into a place of importance when the class content calls for it. When American literary works represent rural people and places in ways that are limited, rural students are in a unique position to call out, to identify, and to lead the class in more sophisticated understandings of these texts. In my attempts to understand my students' disconnect with the academic world and the usefulness of their life experiences, I turned to critical pedagogy. However, despite the clear connection to critical pedagogy, certainly in the sense that I had characterized my students from rural backgrounds as marginalized, somewhat silenced students who are responding to a negative portrayal of themselves in the dominant culture, there are problems with applying critical pedagogy seamlessly to the situation that arises in my classrooms.

Kincheloe's definition of critical pedagogy, which I noted earlier as a pedagogy "interested in the margins of society, the experiences and needs of individuals faced with oppression and marginalization" (*Critical* 23), on the surface seems to provide an entry point from which to explore the empowerment of my rural students. However, a closer examination of the scholarship in this area reveals a series of highly contested terms and approaches that may not operate as hoped for when applied to the student population at Centralia College, because they are not homogenous. They are not all white, or economically challenged, or from a particular religious background, or familiar with animal husbandry. They move constantly between and among identities that are concurrently powerful and powerless.

Compositionists have long had an interest in critical pedagogies that explore the intersection of power, place, and language in the writing classroom. One subfield within composition includes finding moments of critical power for students in the gaps between their experiences and the intellectual tasks they participate in once they enter higher education, and though this seems a promising avenue for possible parallel solutions for rural students, there are unresolved tensions with the theoretical work that has already been completed. It would seem that this work ties marginalization to geographic locations in ways that might also be extended to theories about rural students, but interestingly, these theorists also tend to exclude or minimize the rural in favor of the urban.

Compositionists have explored urban spaces to problematize disconnects for students who come to higher education from urban environments. The city is commonly envisioned in composition studies as the rich site of democratic publics where a diverse population comes into tension as it wrangles with difference in the larger social discourse. Three examples include Paula Mathieu's *Tactics of Hope: The Public Turn in English Composition* (2005), David Fleming's *City of Rhetoric: Revitalizing the Public Sphere in Metropolitan America* (2008), and Bruce McComiskey and Cynthia Ryan's edited collection, *City Comp: Identities, Spaces, Practices* (2003). Fleming's text, in fact, does acknowledge the existence of a space beyond the city, but the rural serves as an oppositional location, and Fleming calls for the city to be "an anchoring social scene capable of helping us invigorate our political lives and develop more centralized, integrated, and equitable public spheres: *commonplaces* that could balance our often-conflicting needs for unity and diversity, accessibility and power, belonging and anonymity" (180). To be fair, the text clearly identifies "contemporary metropolitan North America" (15) as the context and location for a discussion on rhetoric and political and cultural engagement, but Fleming's analysis does not make a connection with rural areas, which seem to be at best an opposing location in his discussion.

Fleming's work highlights the gap between theories that focus on the urban exclusively and the question of how these concerns play out for the issue of engagement in rural areas that I have identified. Fleming argues that "the case study at the heart of this book [Cabrini Green, Chicago] has presented strong evidence for a close relationship between physical location and individual and social welfare in our society and thus good reason to think that place and rhetorical well-being are linked as well" (184). However, if place and rhetorical well-being are linked, they must also be linked in rural environments. For example, Fleming identifies "*density*—the regularity with which community members are thrown into informal contact with one another" (190) as a "rhetorically powerful" (190) factor. But how does density play into rhetorical engagement in rural settings, when people are together repeatedly at family gatherings, religious ceremonies, school sports events, the local grocery store, and the feed store? This is but one example of how compositionists have developed structures of analysis and study of urban locations, and I see their work as useful but not a smooth fit for the students and the context of the rural community college. Therefore, theorists who explore the difficulties for urban students who enter higher education offer only partial help to address my concerns. Other than to suggest a geographic context for marginalized students, their work does not provide much that is directly applicable when working with rural community college students.

Although there is more attention being paid to rural students in the last ten years, prior to that, composition studies paid less attention to the rural as a location from which students bring a knowledge set that may not translate easily and obviously into their experiences in higher education as critical scholars. Students with rural backgrounds whom I have worked with find themselves minimized in higher education, and their personal knowledge may be described by others as irrelevant to the university. As I have pointed out, critical pedagogy provides a lever through which students may be empowered to both create their own critical voices and speak back against oppressive cultural constructs, but, as currently structured, the theory and practice do not quite meet the needs of my students because they are not solely marginalized. As I have previously pointed out, they often occupy multiple positions of power and marginalization at the same time. I hope to address the need to better serve rural students with a special focus on rural students in first- and second-year American literature courses.

There are additional concerns when applying critical pedagogy to rural community college students. Critical pedagogy developed from Paulo Freire's desire to empower Brazil's oppressed peasant students more than fifty years ago, in his book *Pedagogy of the Oppressed* (1968). Freire's targeted students do not match my rural students in a number of important ways, and this causes friction points when utilizing his pedagogical framework with my students in rural Washington State. These points of disconnect are not minor and are similar to the concerns others have raised when working with students who are not Brazilian peasants. First amongst the difficulties is the fact that most of my rural community college students identify with the dominant culture, those Freire labels the oppressors. Those students do not seem to want to see themselves as marginalized or connected to a marginalized group.

There have been numerous attempts by others to parse out how white students, or perhaps students who identify as "white," may not be served well by critical pedagogy. Should these students even be part of the focus in a class that is dominated by critical pedagogy? Is it possible to alter the oppressor through critical pedagogy? And is the oppressor-oppressed binary applicable in all situations? Is it possible in the modern world that students may identify with multiple, overlapping identities in ways that complicated Freire's two options? Is there a way to imagine the aims of critical pedagogy as having relevance for privileged students? For example, older students may have occupied a series of positions in the dominant power structure over the course of their lives. They may have been fully aligned with the powerful dominant culture and then through unemployment, or a geographical move, or a family crisis, lost that position. What part of their identity is still connected with their previous position in society and what part of their identity is co-located with their current, less powerful circumstances? Although critical pedagogy is a well-established methodology in the college classroom, there are points of contention within the theory and practice that illuminate my concerns in using these ideas with rural students who identify with the dominant culture, at least in part, in my American literature survey classes. What follows is a brief overview of these challenges and why using critical pedagogy is not a perfect solution for my concerns yet still stands as a foundational touchstone.

Critical pedagogy does not always empower all students. As bell hooks has repeatedly stated, "privileged students are often downright unwilling to acknowledge that their minds have been colonized, that they have been learning to be oppressors, how to dominate, or at least how to passively accept the domination of others" (102). Supporting her statement, Caleb Corkery's discussion of white racial awareness in Millersville University, Pennsylvania, points out how "critical pedagogies trained on enlightening white students of their privilege are prone to backfire" (250), and I agree. The situation becomes even muddier because my rural students occupy at least two situations concurrently. Most of them are white, a position of racial privilege, and many are also part of a rural subgroup that is routinely marginalized economically and culturally. Corkery advocates for an analytical approach, asking students to approach the hierarchy of power without giving up their privileged position, rather than asking them to engage emotionally with the oppressed, in order to "mitigate student resistance by allowing students to retain their subject positions as they encounter new materials that might challenge their power relations to others" (252).

Critical pedagogy traditionally defined as a method for empowering only "othered" or marginalized students may create barriers when used in my rural community college classroom. Students who align themselves with urban or suburban perspectives, despite their rural backgrounds, might read this approach as hostile. As bell hooks noted, they may not recognize the ways that their acceptance of urban normality and rural marginalization has been deeply engrained by the dominant culture. Rural students, just like other marginalized students, want to place themselves with the powerful, not the powerless, and challenging students' views brings their identities and values into question. I had not considered the seriousness of this challenge to students' worldviews when I pressed students to engage deeply with the literature in my class.

hooks's concerns are explored further, and more specifically with respect to white students, by Jennifer Seibel Trainor. She has concerns about constructions of whiteness that limit white students to racialized conversation that marks them out as the oppressor. She notes that "characterizations [by professors of white students] contribute to static, stereotypical pictures of white, middle class students and their values and beliefs" (632), which leads her to be concerned about a "troubling disdain for students that is anathema to critical pedagogical goals and to the respect for students that has been a core tenet, especially, of composition's disciplinary identity" (632). Trainor's concerns are clearly articulated in two dominant concerns: first, white students in a "multicultural critical pedagogy" become essentialized and politicized in ways that are destructive to the goals of critical pedagogy, and, second, the instructor has created a "rhetorical space" that blocks the possible position of "an antiracist white identity" and therefore limits the ways white students respond to critical texts and pedagogy (634). Trainor's concerns map out areas to which I need to attend. The majority of my students identify along multiple positions of power, so the either/or dichotomy of oppressed or oppressor does not give them a way to explore these concerns of marginalization and power that match their location. As I develop a pedagogy that will be more effective, it is clear that there must be a way for rural students to choose another path, perhaps, as Trainor has suggested, through a white identity that includes being both part of the dominant culture and a marginalized subgroup at the same time.

The concerns that circulate around critical pedagogy when working with white students are related to situations in which a class is led by a white instructor, a generally privileged position. Ricky Lee Allen and César Augusto Rossatto are quite pointed in their concerns about working with white teachers and white teacher-education students. They wonder whether critical pedagogy can be used when the oppressor is the center of the classroom and members of the dominant culture see any questioning of their privileged position as an attack, responding with resistance and at times, hostility (163–65). They raise serious concerns about how critical pedagogy may need an oppressor to operate, and those students who are not marginalized or oppressed must, by default, fall into the oppressor category (165–68). Additionally, students who are not aligned with power have to declare themselves disempowered, marginal, and oppressed, which is perhaps equally alienating to some. Freire's initial construct leaves no room for any person who is a member of the dominant culture, a person with privilege, who is able to shift from that understanding of the world into a position that allows them not only to recognize their privileged status but to act as agents in concert with students who have not had the benefits of privilege.

Additionally, Allen and Rossatto point out situations where powerless students align themselves with the dominant culture to such a degree that "oppressed students might not even believe they are oppressed" (168). Allen and Rossatto's comments bring to mind my own rural students who choose not to engage in the classroom around issues of identity and power. In what ways might I have isolated them, placing them in a tight spot where they have to identify as the marginalized, even to a small degree, when they do not see themselves in this way? Instead, they may be choosing to silence themselves to avoid the conflict, to avoid revealing themselves in this precarious position—or they may not recognize their own expertise in an area that is regarded by the dominant culture as something unimportant.

Allen and Rossatto point out that the driving force behind critical pedagogy, to provide classroom experiences that call into question the power and privilege of the oppressors, may "seem unsuited for privileged geographical and cultural contexts" (170). However, their solutions for this concern do not match the needs of my students. They address situations in which the teacher is white and the students are people of color (174), yet in my classroom nearly all the participants are white. Marginalization is not marked by color, so the power dynamic is, at times, quite difficult to "see," allowing students to ignore or negate the existence of a power hierarchy, at least in the short term of a class discussion. Allen and Rossatto recognize and problematize the difficulties of directing critical pedagogy when the teacher represents a member of the privileged oppressor class with authority over students who are visually and culturally othered. This is not quite the situation on my rural campus, where nearly all professors—93 percent—are white, with a nearly 50-50 split between the genders, and a student body that is 70 percent white. Those students who self-identify in our registration information as Latinx make up 12 percent of the student body ("Faculty and Staff Data"; "Student Demographics").

According to Freire's binary, everyone is a member of either the oppressor or the oppressed group. My community college classroom has a more complicated dynamic. Speaking in agreement with Freire, Allen and Rossatto suggest that there are no "degrees" of oppression, and, given the fluidity of the classroom situation for me, there must be another way to consider the position of these students in the academic world of the community college, a position that occupies multiple locations or degrees of power simultaneously. For example, a white, male student who is living on a farm, who must drive more than ten miles to the college to attend classes and who does not have high-speed internet at home, may also use the campus connections and local high-speed Wi-Fi connections in town or at the homes of friends to participate in multiplayer online games. He may also be related to the largest landowner in the county, a position of significant power in the local community. To ascribe the position of either oppressor or oppressed to this student is to nullify a portion of the student's experiences and identity. In a class discussion, this student needs to draw on multiple positions simultaneously in order to enrich the conversation. Creating activities that allow for students to inhabit multiple locations along a continuum of power and identity is necessary.

Another concern for me is that Allen and Rossatto's solution to a power differential between the white instructor and marginalized students is not well articulated. They rely on repeating Freire's idea of radical love so that oppressor students are "treated as capable of becoming more fully human once released from their investment in the oppressor status" by helping them learn "to not dehumanize themselves and others . . . . And it requires letting them know that if they make a mistake they will still be loved" (178). There are no specifics, and there is problematic language with the embedded statement that white students will make "mistakes," yet these mistakes are not clearly defined or identified. Allen and Rossatto's work illuminates a concern but does not help to alleviate the problem they identify, which to summarize is that instructors who occupy a position of power and cultural dominance may not best serve students who are othered without repeating and replicating the very hegemony they are trying to work against. To minimize an othered student may be an embedded pattern that needs to be addressed, though Allen and Rossatto do not provide clear guidance on just how a disruption of this power dynamic might be accomplished.

Trainor's work, as mentioned earlier, suggests that it is possible to provide a third position for these students. They may legitimately occupy both the oppressed and the oppressor's positions. In the way that students from multiple language communities will code switch, my rural, white students may be daily shifting between these two positions, depending on the needs of the moment. When they are in the feed store, they connect with the marginalized rural, but when they are in the academic world, they connect with the dominant culture. While switching to meet the needs of each audience and identity may be a useful skill, I want these students to enact their knowledge of both these locations, or at least begin to bring those aspects of their lives they consider outside of academic interests, into the classroom. My task, then, in building a critical rural pedagogy, is to find ways to bring the multiple hegemonic positions students occupy into conversation with one another in the classroom. A critical rural pedagogy needs to help all students orient themselves within the broader systems and structures in which they live. A critical rural pedagogy should further help them to see avenues for action and give them opportunities to become aware of and responsible for their own forms of discrimination. A critical rural pedagogy should work with students' already established connections to positions that are both high and low in the power hierarchy. A richer contextualization of their own situations, more complicated than a simple binary, can be explored initially through working with the texts in my American literature classes.

Karen Kopelson's work with student resistance in composition classes suggests students who align themselves with the dominant culture may best be approached with a "performance" pedagogy that casts an image of neutrality, not to sidestep the important work of critical pedagogy, but because a direct assault on the concepts that students use to identify themselves and their place in a larger society may not be effective (118). Kopelson has taken bell hooks's concerns and attempted to devise a way for "oppressor" students to operate within critical pedagogy. For example, students would be encouraged to consider what is and is not oppressive. Students might be asked how to respond and to look outward at an issue/situation to examine multiple formulations of power and its consequences and the various reactions to power.

As I envision it, a critical rural pedagogy then would engage students in the complex thicket of ideas with no clear paths or stark rights and wrongs. Critical rural pedagogy might ask students to unpack, understand, orient, act, and be responsive and responsible for their actions and orientations in the broadest context possible. Traditional critical pedagogy is clearly not the perfected solution to facilitating student growth in areas that are subsumed within the dominant culture's use of education to replicate a current structure at the cost of admittance to power by marginalized students and groups. Because Kopelson's work focuses on minority or marginalized professors and dominantly oppressor students, it does not mirror the situation at my community college, where most of the students are white, and the most frequent markers of marginalization are gender, age, or class. However, she opens a possible set of techniques, a way to create student discussion and outcomes that allow for multiple reactions to the text and their interpretations of that text as it plays out in the world.

The question of student response to critical pedagogy is also tackled by Alexander Reid, and there is some question about whether student resistance to critical pedagogy should be cast as a problem or as an appropriate response to challenges of student identity. Reid proposes that professors consider their own reactions to student resistance (par. 4). Instead of legitimizing an instructor's response based in a perceived lack of some ability, insight, or level of maturity on the part of students, Reid explores the possibility that the power hierarchy of the classroom itself coerces professors to minimize their students' resistance to critical pedagogy (paras 4, 6, and 7). Students should react negatively to a dominating power, in this case the instructor, who attempts to force them into a particular political point of view or a worldview that privileges those who are marginalized. Regardless of the motivation for this move, Reid suggests, when students strongly resist, instructors should see that resistance as a cue, a marker of their own hegemonic control of the classroom. I agree with the concerns he brings to light. Critical pedagogy, as a way to empower those without power, would seem to be incompatible with making students agree with a particular vision of the world in order to please the instructor or to submit to the power structure created by an instructor with a particular agenda. Reid's concerns in this area clearly identify a significant point of friction within critical pedagogy. However, they also suggest that a variation in critical pedagogy that places students in a role of some power may break through their resistance to participating fully and validate their contributions of (in my case, rural) knowledge to classroom discussions.

Clearly, although there are important ideas relating to rural students and their sense of place within the world of higher education as well as how the hegemony of the urban or suburban as the "normal" or more familiar lens might marginalize or minimize rural students who are in community colleges, at this time these concerns have had only limited discussion in academic conversations. I believe other scholars have outlined the concerns, which I will discuss more fully in Chapter 2, both in terms of hegemony and the creation of a rural identity. For now, suffice it to say, the terms *rural literacy* and *rural pedagogy* are contested both in their definitions and in their uses, which reflects the difficulties in attempting to build on the work of earlier scholars to create a critical rural pedagogy. However, what I next wish to explore more fully is how specific representations of the rural, as rhetorical commonplaces or topoi, that circulate within literature and in public discourse have been internalized by students (and their professors) and how such topoi might be used strategically in what I am calling a critical rural pedagogy in order to examine, challenge, resist, and intervene within these representations.

The Topoi: Commonplace Representations of the Rural in Dominant Culture

The approach I take begins with already established formulations of the rural that circulate in the social imagination and are replicated in American literary texts and in the ancillary materials that precede these texts in American literature anthologies. The imagery of the rural in the literature we study in class may be a part of what silences students from rural backgrounds who do not wish to be associated with marginalized groups, e.g., country people, or representations that diminish the value of their lives since they are not part of the urban or suburban worlds. I envision using the imagery and characterizations of the rural as lever points against which to compare rural students' experiences, to build patterns of argument that can break down these ideas more critically. In their idealized form, these representations are commonplaces—concepts, symbols, or key words connected to the ideals of a "rural" world—and recognizing them as such can serve as a way into analyzing and dissecting them, which will give rural students more agency than they currently experience in my classroom.

I hope to repurpose those dominant representations as a basis for resistance, a strategy I first saw enacted in critical pedagogy. As Gerald Graff and Cathy Birkenstein explain in *They Say / I Say: The Moves That Matter in Academic Writing*, "public orators from ancient Greece and Rome through the European Renaissance studied rhetorical *topoi* or 'commonplaces,' model passages and formulas that represented the different strategies available to public speakers" (xxii). As Aristotle originally articulated, a topos is "a mental 'place' where an argument can be found, or topoi may be the argument itself" (44–45). Another way to think about topoi is that they are based in "common warrants, often unstated premises that seek to connect with an audience's hierarchy of values, and several studies have evidenced their power as inventional tools for students" (Wilder and Wolfe 174). Topoi are these commonly held beliefs and understandings that provide a starting point for more complicated analysis. A culturally constructed set of ideas about what the rural is, what it represents, and what the value of "rural" is in the larger context of the nation might serve as an "in." This is a way to challenge the "idea of the rural" in order to reveal the more complicated reality of the rural that my students have lived and understand. Because my students have experiences that help them recognize the distinctions between these culturally constructed representations and the reality of life in rural locations, a class with rural students can use their collective knowledge to push back against these commonplaces, using, for example, the idea that the rural is merely a rustic, backwater location as a point of contrast with the rural that students know directly through their experiences.

I understand that the repeated images and assumptions that circulate in literature, public discourse, and popular sentiment on the rural are topoi, and I aim to help students both recognize and mobilize these topoi in complicated and multilayered ways. I have chosen this term specifically to describe the moves I want to make with students because it encapsulates the shifting nature of the discovery of critical argument as well as the structures that can be used to facilitate student exploration of these issues to a greater depth. As stated by Sharon Crowley and Debra Hawhee, topoi have been deployed as "both the stuff of which arguments are made and the form of those arguments" (152). Although there are multiple ways topoi function, I will be focused most closely on Candice Rai's more specific explanation, in which topoi are also "the reified tools, material conditions and mechanisms (objects, things, spaces, genres, bodily habits, and other materialities) that constrain, enact, generate, circulate, and mobilize salient rhetorical structures" (36–37). Topoi are not merely stock discursive structures to be used. They rise out of specific conditions, contain contradictory worldviews and beliefs, and provide spaces for interaction with contentious ideas that are alive at this moment in the culture or in this case a specific subculture.

Similarly, Ralph Cintron conceptualizes "topoi (commonplaces) as storehouses of social energy. . . . topoi organize our sentiments, beliefs, and actions in the lifeworld" (101). I agree with his assertion that topoi "constitute the body politic in a visible and highly public sort of way" (101). The representations of the rural my students have internalized are already part of a widely understood cultural conversation and, regardless of students' specific individual backgrounds, attention to topoi provides not only the means by which to deconstruct the power structures, political agendas, and cultural impulses embedded in them, but also the means to speak back, to create rhetorical responses that have salience and power. Additionally, by identifying these representations as topoi, rural students are provided with a way to bring their personal knowledge into the academic world in ways that are in line with academic expectations and concurrently demonstrate the importance of multiple perspectives being voiced in the university. Also, recognizing representations of the rural as topoi may allow the discovery of ideas that rural students need to be able to develop for themselves in order to occupy multiple hegemonic locations between the dominant culture and the marginalized rural. I will discuss more fully how and why topoi will be enacted as part of a critical rural pedagogy in Chapter 2.

In order to use representations of the rural as topoi to be interrogated with rural students in my classes, it is important to clearly determine the prevalence of these particular images of and attitudes toward the rural. Because repeated rural representations function as topoi, ideas that have deep resonance with the larger culture and are reflected in the written works students and scholars encounter, they can be used in my classroom as structures for conversation, activities, analysis, and tools of invention that help generate content for writing. Topoi can provide a way for my rural students, who will recognize that these topoi do not encompass the totality of their experiences in a rural environment, to question the purposes of rural representations in texts for the author, for the reader, and for other groups who may have either political or cultural reasons for promoting specific views of the rural in literature. As Rai, Cintron, and Crowley and Hawhee point out, topoi are the content of representations of the rural that students may articulate and examine, as well as the tools that help them to question, to push back, and to mobilize as they explore texts in American literature. Furthermore, if constructed images of the rural and its people are culturally dominant, and if rural students can be made aware of them, they might use them to push back critically against the texts.

Students who have not had agricultural experiences must not be isolated or minimized by a pedagogy that focuses too exclusively on a homogenous vision of the rural. Because my students have usually come from a variety of backgrounds, including not just rural but suburban and urban locations, this is especially important. Culturally dominant representations of the rural must operate as warrants, as common assumptions, so that students who do not have direct experiences in the rural are still familiar with the topoi and able to engage and interrogate them, and for the purposes of this book, keying in on three repeated, general, and common constructions of the rural may help students learn to recognize the overgeneralization and political hierarchy that is imposed by these representations of the rural.

The work of Kim Donehower, Charlotte Hogg, and Eileen E. Schell on rural literacies within composition studies, which I will discuss in more detail later in this chapter and in Chapter 2, might be used strategically in a classroom that aims to use the experiences of rural students to engage in critical analysis of texts in my American literature courses. Donehower, Hogg, and Schell have explored the prevalence of language and attitudes in dominant culture that marginalize rural places and people. In *Rural Literacies* (2007), they call for a closer examination of the traditional misrepresentation of rural places as locations for only "lack, lag, and a rosy past" (1). These misrepresentations assert that the rural is missing important economic or cultural attributes, is slow to follow the improvements of urbanized neighbors, or is the site of sweet memories of a fictional farm life where daily tasks are easy, simple, and character building. According to Donehower, Hogg, and Schell, these misrepresentations may be found individually, in a pair, or all three together in the same work. I would assert that these three representations are shifting. For example, representation of the rural as a location for a "rosy past" will be explored, enacted, articulated, and privileged or not differently within multiple texts. It is not enough for students to point to an example of rosy past. Instead, by using rosy past as a topos, the multilayered use of this term, the variation in its expression, and the full range of possible cultural meanings that are associated with it should be included in a critical rural pedagogy.

Next, I look at how these concepts play out when framed as topoi, or rhetorical commonplaces, keywords and ideological formations that circulate in the discourse of the classroom, in literature, in social spaces, and in the everyday lives of my students. Through the tracing and strategic use of these topoi, students may begin to understand how the images and representations in a work of literature do not reflect an absolute reality but instead create merely one author's vision of rural places, a vision that reflects ideological dispositions that may or may not have clear connections with rural life. As topoi, these three representations of rural places provide a jumping-off point for students as they interrogate the extent to which rural spaces are or are not places that lack cultural and economic resources available in urban spaces, as places that are or are not behind in their cultural and economic development, or as places that represent an idealized, and perhaps fictionalized, past for urbanites (Donehower et al., *Rural Literacies* 1). Because topoi are dynamic and capacious, they serve well to capture the shifting nature of rural representations. Because there are myriad, contested ways that lack, lag, or rosy past are enacted in these rural representations, students will need to delve repeatedly into how the representation of the rural is altered and how it evolves from one text to another. I can use these topoi as a framework for a critical rural pedagogy that calls all students to examine how representations of the rural may be revealed, obscured, altered, and created.

Lack, Lag, and Rosy Past: Connections with the Field

Donehower, Hogg, and Schell's identification of "lack, lag, and rosy past" is strongly connected to the work of previous scholars who focus on the rural. These three general representations also appear with regularity in popular literature, memoirs, and even United States government publications. These common representations are repeatedly used to further their own agendas by those who do not live and work in rural areas. Urban dwellers may scapegoat or oversimplify the rural to create an illusion of the superiority of cities, politicians may use a rural-versus-urban dichotomy to influence policy development, and those who have left a rural environment for an urban one may want to depict their choice as liberation from a diminished location and lifestyle.

What follows is a brief review of literary, popular, and government texts that replicate the ideas and imagery of "lack, lag, and rosy past." In order to illustrate the pervasive nature of these three representations of the rural, it is important to demonstrate that representations appear nearly ubiquitously in multiple genres in order to be sure that I can construct a form of critical pedagogy that will work with and against these representations later in Chapter 2. I will include the following texts to explore the scholarly conversation about the rural as it appears in American literature: F. O. Matthiessen's *American Renaissance*, Anna Brickhouse's *Transamerican Literary Relations and the Nineteenth-Century Public Sphere*, A. Carl Bredahl's *New Ground*, Henry Nash Smith's *Virgin Land: The American West as Symbol and Myth*, and Leo Marx's *Machine in the Garden*. I will follow that with the work of urban and social planners with designs on the rural, Deborah E. Popper and Frank J. Popper. Next, scholars who explore geographic theory and writing, Brückner and Hsuan L. Hsu, Robert E. Abrams, Mary Louise Pratt, and Allen Batteau are glossed. Lack, lag, or rosy past also appear in federal government documents, genres which often catalogue, characterize, and control rural land and peoples to an astounding degree, and in several Kellogg Foundation reports for Congress. Finally, I will include a scan of literature/

memoir/popular texts by Ian Frazier, Wendell Berry, Osha Gray Davidson, NPR contributors Peggy Lowe and Ted Robbins, and Michael Pollan. It is not my intention to use these specific texts as classroom examples as part of this book. Rather, I will be looking closely at the ways the representations of lack, lag, and rosy past, and the ways rural spaces are controlled in texts by outsiders, occur repeatedly, across genres. The frequency of this repetition validates recognizing and critiquing "lack, lag, and rosy past" as pervasive topoi in our culture. The constant drumbeat of these images helps to illustrate my confidence in using them with my rural students, who will also recognize these representations when encountered in American literature texts and supplementary materials.

All my students should also be familiar with these constructions of the rural, and if lack, lag, and rosy past are truly in the dominant culture, these students will also learn to recognize the gap between the constructed world of a text and the actual world being described. Because my students have experiences with rural living, with small-town culture, or with more frequent interactions with rural life realities, they should recognize how these two different worlds are in accord with one another at times and how they are more complicated in their distinctions across contexts when they engage in exploring the topoi of lack, lag, and rosy past. When these experiences are shared in the classroom, all students have access to information and points of view that help them to discern the layers of meaning and purpose in their American literature texts. These skills are important for the empowerment of all students. While limitations of time and space preclude me from analyzing all possible texts, I have attempted to use a variety of texts to illustrate the frequency and often uncritical use of these topoi in scholarly texts, popular fiction, and political documents. The repeated use of lack, lag, and rosy past in all their variations suggests that they are firmly embedded in dominant American culture. And if they are firmly embedded, they can be used as topoi for critical interrogation of texts with students.

Scholarly Context for the Rural in American Literature

Images of the rural in American literary works have been at times a focus of scholarly attention and at other times granted only a minimal discussion, but the question of how, why, and for whom rural spaces appear in American literature has a long history. I will attempt to highlight several examples of scholars of American literature who theorize and problematize the way the American rural appears, or not, and how it is constructed through literature within the conversation, realizing that a full discussion is beyond the scope of my project. I do so in order to trace the academic conversation on when, how, and why images of the rural are created and manipulated in literature, and to clarify the repeated use of lack, lag, and rosy past as topoi that can be used in classroom settings to complicate students' understandings of texts in general, and of texts that include references and images of a marginalized rural, specifically. So my aim is not to be comprehensive but representative in the presentation of rural topoi. It is important that I demonstrate a repeated and common use of lack, lag, and rosy past as they occur at times separately, at times together. I will begin with discussions of American literature since the class that is the impetus for this project and that will be the point of intervention is a general American literature survey.

F. O. Matthiessen, in his introduction to *American Renaissance: Art and Expression in the Age of Emerson and Whitman* (1941), asserts that Emerson, Hawthorne, Thoreau, Whitman, and Melville both reflect and create a particular type of democracy in their texts (xv). Interestingly, Matthiessen is uncritical in his glancing descriptions of the rural and his assertion that between 1850 and 1865 "the farmer rather than the businessman was still the average American" (ix). This, he suggests, helps to support the major writers of the day in their use of natural imagery, which he often conflates with rural imagery without distinction. Matthiessen's terminology is still in use today, and Brickhouse pushes back against the general creation of a dominant white male canon in *Transamerican Literary Relations and the Nineteenth-Century Public Sphere* (2004). Expanding the boundaries of Matthiessen's conception of American literature, she argues that "the very conception of the American Renaissance, tied as it has always been to a cultural moment of intense national self-consciousness, is inherently dependent upon and sustained not only by nationalist discourses but by the underlying transnational desires and anxieties that such discourses seek to mask" (33). Brickhouse foregrounds important binaries, including us (Anglo-Saxon) versus them (native, Spanish, not from northern Europe) (4), and the national identity-literature of the United States when held against "colonialism, slavery, and indigenous 'removals'" (9). She does not, however, include a rural-urban binary or distinction among her critical turns, which suggests that not only is the rural of minimal importance, but it is not part of the development of the nineteen-century public world she is describing. The rural does not seem to matter, despite the significant number of people who were living in rural areas of the United States all through the 1800s.

A. Carl Bredahl also asserts that the construction of the American literary canon, a highly problematic term and concept, privileges the Eastern, but he adds, more specifically, the urban. In *New Ground: Western American Narrative and the Literary Canon* (1989), he notes a distinction between the way Easterners and Westerners understand landscape and the stories placed in those landscapes. He writes, "Not surprisingly, traditional students, trained to distrust surface, frequently regard western writing as naïve. But . . . distant from eastern structures and challenged by the big sky, the westerner finds himself accepting the landscape and indeed embracing it for physical and spiritual sustenance" (30). Rural spaces and small towns, with an abundance of sky and landscape, are not central to the canon, according to Bredahl, not because they do not have value, but because those in positions of power have minimized their value for the sake of placing the complexities of urban life above all other contexts. Bredahl's work describes how the canon diminishes inclusion of western/rural locations in "American" literature. My experiences with students suggest that they understand this hegemonic structure and have internalized it to the point that they may not value their experiences and knowledge because they perceive them to be not as academically fit or rigorous. In the words of Bredahl, their lives and knowledge are "naïve" in the context of an American literature survey course. And there is danger in challenging "America's perception of itself" (32), as Bredahl points out. When confronted with a powerful set of urban images, which are given greater worth both in American literary texts and in the dominant culture, it seems that rural students in my classes may choose to disappear, not to challenge, not to question, and to stay safe in an environment that may be hostile to their success if they privilege the rural or nonurban in their literary analysis and critiques. As illustrated in the opening vignette, they elect to remain silent and choose not to bring their expert knowledge of rural life and spaces into discussions of American literature. The danger of not being recognized as a valued member of the academic community, let alone a person with opinions that are valuable in classroom discussions, is avoided if a student simply does not bring their knowledge out in the open.

Other scholars have given rural representations a more dominant place in their theorizing. Henry Nash Smith traces shifts in imagery surrounding "domesticated" rural spaces in *Virgin Land* (1957), developing the idea that

> the interior of the continent became one of the dominant symbols of nineteenth-century American society—a collective representation, a poetic idea (as Tocqueville noted in the early 1830's) that defined the promise of American life. . . . [T]he garden embraced a cluster of metaphors expressing fecundity, growth, increase, and blissful labor in the earth, all centering about the heroic figure of the idealized frontier farmer armed with that supreme agrarian weapon, the sacred plow. (138)

Smith made areas outside of urban spaces a metaphorical conception rather than a realistic vision, which enabled a fictional image to develop, an "agricultural paradise in the West, embodying group memories of an earlier, a simpler, and, it was believed, a happier state of society" (139). While Smith's idealized frontier farmer parallels the idea of a rosy past exemplified in the rural, and his title certainly mirrors the lack of interaction with the natural world in rural spaces, he does not focus on the concept of a culturally or economically lagging location, illustrating that these rural representations may appear individually as well as in pairs or all together. Certainly, the overt construction of this imagery, and the degree to which Smith is responding directly to the industrialization of urban areas, lays the theoretical groundwork on which Donehower, Hogg, and Schell later point out how rural places become locations for only "lack, lag, and a rosy past" (*Rural Literacies* 1). Smith points to the importance of the rosy past in the initial development of an American character and then its continued dominance into the modern age. He refers both to Thomas Jefferson's conception of the yeoman farmer and to J. Hector St. John Crèvecoeur's *Letters from an American Farmer*, two texts that stand as antecedents to Nash's continued development of the theoretical framework (142).

Leo Marx's work, *The Machine in the Garden* (1964), opens with, "The pastoral ideal has been used to define the meaning of America ever since the age of discovery, and it has not yet lost its hold upon the native imagination" (3). I will withhold commentary on his use of the term "native" to refer to dominant white culture but will instead note that Marx foregrounds what it means to be an American as reflected in the landscape people inhabit, and how these developing representations may be altered when pastoral locations experience urbanizing technologies. He makes powerful use of the historical extensions of train lines and engines as objects that appear in important American literary works. Marx traces the use of pastoral imagery in literature back to the European Romantics and then even further to the Roman poet Virgil. However, he also makes unquestioned statements, such as that "the soft veil of nostalgia that hangs over our urbanized landscape is largely a vestige of the once dominant image of an undefiled, green republic, a quiet land of forests, villages, and farms dedicated to the pursuit of happiness" (6).

For Marx, the rural is a domesticated space to be leveraged against the industrialization of the United States. He leans toward an idealized version of spaces outside of cities that are most useful as points of contrast rather than as sites with their own complicated history and use. My rural students who have often been awake since well before dawn to care for livestock and who know the constant stress of a never-ending list of daily and seasonally repeated chores that must be completed in order to keep a farmstead in profitable status would certainly disagree with Marx's nostalgic characterization of the rural. My purpose then should be to encourage students to analyze these differences between the rural as portrayed and the rural as they have lived it, including individual variations of their unique experiences in the rural, a subject that I will explore more deeply in Chapter 2 and then express in practical terms in Chapter 3.

Stepping even more overtly toward controlling the rural with text, social planners with designs on the rural Deborah E. Popper and Frank J. Popper wrote an especially influential 1999 article, "The Buffalo Commons: Metaphor as Method," that illustrates how urban peoples' vision serves the urban rather than rural inhabitants. Their stated aim is to "craft regional metaphors. . . . [that] can help the public to understand and expand regional choices. As a metaphor for the United States' Great Plains, the Buffalo Commons stand for a large-scale, long-term ecological-economic restoration project" (491). They describe the Great Plains as "America's steppes—wind-swept, nearly treeless, and largely semiarid. Their expanse is mostly rural and sparsely settled" (491–92). For the Poppers, population density endows value, a value judgment that gives greater power to the urban. Their proposed "public policy for the Plains would eventually have to respond . . . by creating a huge reserve, the Buffalo Commons" (493). In summary, since the Great Plains cannot sustain large populations over long periods of time, ownership should be taken by the federal government (493). The government would then use these lands as a reserve for buffalo, also known as bison, an endangered species. For the Poppers, spaces outside of cities are empty spaces, lacking in sustainable value.

Shifting to literary scholars who focus more specifically on the intersection of geography and written works, that rural locations are altered in text to meet particular needs is not disputed by literary theorists. My work with students using topoi to reveal motives and power structures within texts is grounded in the work of these theorists. Geographical space is pliable in the writer's skilled hands, molded into the form and representations of specific ideas, according to Martin Brückner and Hsuan L. Hsu, editors of *American Literary Geographies: Spatial Practice and Cultural Production 1500–1900* (2007). In their introduction, they foreground the writer's ability to "transform the literary stage from the homogeneous space of an expansive democratic empire to a multitude of qualitatively different spaces that varied significantly from prominent discourses in the history of human consciousness and emotions" (13). They highlight, specifically, Frederick Jackson Turner's use of the frontier as a place in which "America's sense of national identity . . .[and] democratic individualism had been continually forged" (14). Brückner and Hsu agree that the understanding of space is controlled by the imagery that is developed for an audience. In their study of maps and railroad company advertising, they demonstrate repeatedly how space may be homogenized or divided into distinct images based on the needs of the authors of those maps and texts.

Robert E. Abrams, in *Landscape and Ideology in American Renaissance Literature: Topographies of Skepticism* (2004), concurs with the supposition that physical locations are malleable when re-created by authors and artists. He points out that in capturing images, in this case in paintings by Thomas Cole as well as images developed by American writers from the same historical period, "what emerges is a drift in concrete material possibility through ongoing mutation in the socio-cultural mechanisms whereby it is measured and endowed with value, semioticized into symbol and sign, mapped, categorized, and formulated to the eye" (127). Again, the constructed understanding of a space is made plain in this work as in that of Brückner and Hsu. The representations of space that appear in text are not a singular truth of a place that is faithfully recorded without the author's perspective and the cultural influences that play out in writers' lives. Instead, geographical spaces in texts are built, they have a purpose that is not isolated from the time and purposes of the authors, and they reflect but one way to take a reader to a place and time. Representations of the rural that appear in the American literature survey course are subject to the same influences. Because my students have personal experiences that may help them to recognize the differences between what they know about the rural and how the rural is depicted, there is an opportunity for critical analysis. It is my hope to use this theoretical underpinning to develop both a critical stance and a critical pedagogy for use with rural students when they are confronting images created in their American literature textbooks.

One especially powerful example of the deliberate manipulation of representations of the rural to create a particular response is found in Allen Batteau's *The Invention of Appalachia* (1990). Batteau's first sentence states, "Appalachia is a creature of the urban imagination" (1). He then spends the following two hundred pages providing specific examples of how people outside of Appalachia ranging from Thomas Jefferson and Crèvecoeur to filmmakers, musicians, novelists, and television producers have invented a particular version of life in this multistate area in order to achieve their own purposes. The rural parts of Appalachia are used for political gain, urban solidarity, and consolidation of power by those who wish to control the area. The invention of a people who lag behind in education and culture, who lack the modern conveniences, and who represent a version of a storied past that has gone awry because it could not adjust to the present, modern world, according to Batteau, has been developed to serve those who wish to use the rural for their own purposes. The creators of Appalachia construct a rural space that needs to be "filled" with superior urban economic wisdom and culture.

Clearly, the academic conversation around the rural as it appears in scholarly works suggests that there is ample evidence for a pattern of representations that diminish the importance and relevance of the rural, at times creating a rosy version of it. When the rural is overgeneralized into one or more of the three general topoi identified by Donehower, Hogg, and Schell, there are patterns for students to discover and opportunities to create situations for rural community college students to use their perspectives to contest the accuracy of these representations.

A diminished value of the rural becomes a greater concern when considered in light of Mary Louis Pratt's conception of the "contact zone . . . that is, social spaces where disparate cultures meet, clash, and grapple with each other, often in highly asymmetrical relations of domination and subordination" (7). The unequal power structure is fully apparent, with the rural subjected to the colonizing gaze of the urban. Pratt's terms may also be useful to investigate how students who have lived in these rural contact zones may engage in "autoethnographic expression" to "talk back" to the dominating powers outside of their communities (9). Talking back is critically important because it is a mechanism for students from rural spaces to use their expertise with the rural to develop their own critical thinking skills, as well as add to the richness of ideas present in their college classrooms. In my exploration of possible pedagogies, Pratt's work suggests that providing avenues for students to represent themselves back to the colonizer, in this case the urban normative assumption, helps to explain why rural students try to ally themselves with Freire's oppressors, in this case the nonrural creator of rural representations, while concurrently these same students are cast among the oppressed in Freire's binary. Calling out the assumption that the urban is normal at the same time creates a tool through which rural students can work. Taking a cue from critical pedagogy, there is a way to create assignments and opportunities for students to rewrite the texts with their own knowledge, using the urban language of lack, lag, and rosy past as a foil against which to work or to develop counternarratives.

Talking back is a pathway to creating more nuanced responses to texts in American literature. By talking back, students resist the colonizing gaze of authors who have a particular economic, political, or cultural agenda when writing about the rural. Tactically, using Pratt's theories as a guide, there are specific tasks that can be built on talking back that give students a foothold in their critical reactions and responses even to texts that are held in esteem because they appear in a college classroom or in an assigned anthology. In Chapter 2, I will explore pedagogy that tackles concerns for rural students and how I can build on it for my students' specific situations. For example, when the Poppers' colonizing gaze ascribes lack to the entire open plains, the West and the Middle West, students can work directly against that representation. Since the Poppers define the rural as nonproductive and empty, students might begin to push back by identifying what is in the rural landscape and how it is divided and used according for specific economic and cultural purposes by multiple groups of people who inhabit the geographic space. They can explore the people that the Poppers have marginalized to the point of extinction, and their interactions with the land and with one another. Such an activity may even include direct contact with the Poppers in the form of a report, a letter, or a response that refutes the assumptions in their original article. As stated before, although critical pedagogy engages marginalized students in their need to become empowered and respond to texts in their own voices, it does not match my classroom needs completely. Because rural students in my classes may not identify themselves as marginalized, I need to develop a possible set of pedagogical moves that combine the ideas of Donehower, Hogg, and Schell with those of Pratt and critical pedagogy.

How a space is contextualized and discussed can have a powerful impact on the way those from outside a space respond. This idea has been deeply demonstrated by multiple scholarly works, but with respect to the ways that rural and small-town locations have been defined and represented in writing, there is a nearly endless supply of examples that one can draw on in order to support my assertion that the themes of lack, lag, and rosy past are common and, therefore, familiar to all students, not just rural students. However, I would like to point out just a few of the other genres of texts that capture the colonizing gaze of the authors when describing the rural.

United States Government Constructs the Rural in Government Materials

Commonly, people with an urban orientation are unaware of the powerful control exerted by governmental agencies on rural spaces, peoples, and activities. Rural spaces, including farmland, ranchland, and public grazing tracts are defined and organized by governmental and quasigovernmental agencies. The National Park Service, the Farm Bureau, the Department of Agriculture, and even the US Census, to name but a few of these organizations, not only determine what can be called rural but what activities may occur in those locations: when and which crops are planted, who may have access to various types of rural spaces, what property must be held in land banks, and how products of the rural environment may be planned, created, marketed, and at times, destroyed. In short, the government has a profound influence on daily life in the rural. This is clearly visible for people living and working in rural spaces. But this is not apparent to those outside of the rural.

I will share two documents that illustrate how policymakers and regulators, and those who elect them, reflect the ideas of lack, lag, or rosy past. The strength of these beliefs, attitudes, or impressions of the rural are then enacted in the laws and bureaucratic texts that govern rural spaces. Not only rural students but suburban and urban students should be aware of how these representations become "real" in government actions carried out by their fellow citizens.

Two reports compiled by the W. K. Kellogg Foundation, written in 2002 for the US Congress, attempt to document perceptions of the rural. The first report, *Perceptions of Rural America: Congressional Perspectives*, made public in May 2002, was a "bi-partisan survey [that] included 26 members of Congress," sixteen of whom were Democratic house members and senators and ten of whom were Republican house members and senators (2). The second report, *Perceptions of Rural America* (December 2002) was developed from "242 in-depth interviews of rural, urban, and suburban Americans in several regions of the country" (1).

The perspectives identified in the report on the legislators' views use the term "lack" repeatedly; rural America is described have having a "lack of economic diversity . . . lack of infrastructure . . . lack of access to the Internet and inadequate transportation" (2). The area falls behind the rest of the United States in solutions to these problems because the rural economy needs to improve, when compared with the urban and suburban economy, and rural areas may have fewer representatives in Congress, potentially meaning less power and influence in governmental policy development, especially in terms of the Farm Bill (2). Interestingly, the legislators see rural communities "as an incubator of American values, such as self-reliance, stewardship of the land and faith, [and] it represents an important source of American tradition" (2), paralleling the idealization of the rural described by Donehower, Hogg, and Schell as the rosy past. Again, the Kellogg report does not record the reality of these terms but instead reveals and reinforces dominant perceptions in the minds of elected national government representatives, and since members of Congress are writing policy, proposing legislation, and establishing funding, their perceptions percolate strongly throughout federal programs, which rural students often know in detail. Those who have power "see" with Pratt's colonizers' gaze.

Government research also suggests similar perceptions from American citizens outside of Congress. The second report reveals similar perceptions by a sample of Americans and then contrasts these perceptions with collected data. In summation, the report states:

> This means that perceptions of rural America are centered on a series of dichotomies—rural life represents traditional American values, but is behind the times; rural life is more relaxed and slower than city life, but harder and more grueling; rural life is friendly but intolerant of outsiders and difference; and rural life is richer in community life, but epitomized by individuals struggling independently to make ends meet. (1)

The fact that these perceptions are not accurate when compared with the data gathered about rural America is highlighted in the report.

The misperceptions identified in these reports are also reflected in rural students' awareness of a disconnect between what rural life "really" is and how it is perceived by others. Recently, during the "passing" time between classes, a heated discussion began when a student who raises and shows hogs, and is an active member of the Future Farmers of America, began to verbalize his excitement about going to a national FFA conference. He was especially excited that he was going to be with people who would understand his farm circumstances immediately. As he began to complain about urbanites' misconceptions about farm life, several other students chimed in. They spoke together with great vigor for the remaining five minutes before class started. However, when I attempted to transition their discussion into a relevant topic during official class time, they were universally resistant. This class moment reinforces my belief that students from rural backgrounds already recognize and could use these dominant images of the lack, lag, and rosy past paradigm as jumping-off points, topoi to push back against, to isolate elements of, or to interrogate in the texts they read in their American literature.

Cultural Context, Popular Fiction, and Popular Texts

Finally, I trace Donehower, Hogg, and Schell's three representations, lack, lag, and rosy past, as topoi that appear in popular texts and public discourse. There are certainly numerous books that treat nonurban spaces with Pratt's colonizing eye. For example, Ian Frazier's *Great Plains* (1989) is a travelogue. The memoir traces the author's travels from the urban Eastern United States out into the West, a place that he first needs to define, to identify boundaries for, and then replicate for the readers of his book, complete with fascinating and little-known details. Frazier repeatedly identifies what is lacking in the landscape:

> I didn't pass a single place that looked as if it was in any way expecting me: no landscaped residential communities, no specialty sporting-goods stores, no gourmet delis offering many kinds of imported beers. Just grain silos, and flat, brown fields with one cow on them, and wheat fields, and telephone poles, and towns with four or six buildings and a "No U-Turn" sign at each end. (10)

Frazier's intended audience is primarily Eastern urbanites who can travel to this foreign space through his book. The book is littered with travelogue details, somewhat humorous adventures, and the author's wry voice, at once both enchanted with this landscape and distinctly separate from it. He was a traveler to an exotic place, whose representation he controls and reproduces in his memoir.

When my students read portions of Frazier's memoir, they seem to universally align themselves with Frazier, despite the fact that some of them are closer in their experiences to the people who inhabit his landscape. Conversation does not go willingly into a space where Frazier's depictions are questioned, despite my attempt to pull students in that direction. Clearly, my previous strategies have not been adequate to the task. Students comment on the funny characters, choosing not to share their familiarity with rural people or unable to separate themselves from the dominant culture's clearly preferred position.

Initially, I expected to find less marginalizing in the works of Wendell Berry, a well-known conservation advocate who encourages living in rural spaces in his texts. In his collection, *The Art of the Commonplace: The Agrarian Essays of Wendell Berry* (2002), Berry locates "Agrarianism" within the conservation movement, both connecting with rural agricultural practices and arguing against diminishing the experience of life in rural or nonindustrial areas. However, after closer examination it is clear he lays out theoretical groundwork that reinforces the construction of rural places as lacking. Berry also uses a falsely constructed narrative. When he waxes poetic about the binary of woods and cultivated, domesticated fields, he omits previous inhabitants in order to perpetuate a metaphor of a pristine, untouched land. He chides the urban visitor to rural spaces who leaves beer cans and killed animals behind for being "the true American pioneer, perfectly at rest in his assumption that he is the first and the last whose inheritance and fate this place will ever be" (22). He refers to the way white settlers "undertook the privilege of the virgin abundance of this land. . . . And to come to that understanding it is necessary, even now, to leave the regions of our conquest—the cleared fields, the towns and cities, the highways—and re-enter the woods" (26–27). Berry wants to create a vision of geographic space on which particular work reinforces hegemony, a power structure that simply does not reflect the reality that the land was occupied prior to white settlers. He reinforces the binary of domesticated space or empty woodlands, which forms the heart of his Agrarian construct. The world he builds fits his purposes, so it must erase Native Americans, women, and people of color who may have inhabited or currently inhabit the landscape.

The marginalization of the rural is familiar enough in the dominant culture that Osha Gray Davidson, author of *Broken Heartland* (1990), used the imagery as a certainty he could work against. He wrote:

> To most Americans, rural communities are just dim blurs alongside the gleaming superhighway that carries us into what we tell ourselves is an ever-brighter future. If we notice those blurs at all, it is usually to laugh at their quaintness, perhaps

> warmly à la writer and humorist Garrison Keillor, or to shake our heads at the backwardness of our unfortunate rural cousins. Few, however, slow down enough to allow the blurs to differentiate themselves into real people, in real communities, with real problems to be solved or ignored. Time has not forgotten Keillor's Lake Wobegon; we have. (Davidson 71)

Davidson's rural spaces are so missing, so lacking, that they are quite literally unseen. They are just hazy spots that flash by when one drives down a highway. This concerns me in this book because Davidson depicts my rural students' experiences as outside the normal, invisible in the happening of the world where power and decision-making take place. This seems a powerful message to my students to stay quiet because they are not important, not even worth noticing. And my observations up to this point suggest my students have learned this lesson all too well.

And to add another example of how lack, lag, and rosy past have become uncritically embedded in recent popular cultural representations of the rural, National Public Radio ran two stories on January 23, 2013, that focused on rural topics. The first was an exposé demonstrating tomato growers' challenges from Mexican tomato growers dumping their product on the American market at below-market prices. Gary Hufbauer, a senior fellow with the Peterson Institute for International Economics in Washington, DC, pulled out a "rosy past" reference to make his point. He explained, "[T]he mental image of the little house on the prairie has most of us captivated in Florida" and he finishes the comparison between Florida's agribusiness industry by saying that "the little house on the prairie is a tomato grower, a sugar grower, or an orange grower—a small part of the economy, but a big part of the popular imagination" (qtd. in Robbins). Agribusiness is in no way similar to the small homesteaders depicted in the *Little House on the Prairie* books by Laura Ingalls Wilder, but the image works to Hufbauer's advantage and is readily accepted by the NPR audience. The second NPR piece reported on a dairy farmer cooperative in the Southeast United States that had actually become a milk monopoly, to the financial detriment of cooperative members. A lawsuit was filed, and in describing the details, NPR reporter Peggy Lowe wrote that "the deal makes the milk industry icon Elsie the Cow look instead like Gordon Gekko." The urban-rural binary is clearly in play, and Lowe's comparison relies on an audience familiar with the mythologized vision of farming in order to complete her image.

In Michael Pollan's 2006 bestseller, *The Omnivore's Dilemma: A Natural History of Four Meals*, Pollan attempts to follow food from the point of origin to the grocery store or restaurant. Interestingly, the general public's misunderstanding of farming is so profound that Pollan has to spend the first four chapters of his book, eighty-five pages, explaining the physical and economic realities of current farming practices. He relied on the expected representations of lack, lag, and rosy past, and then used them as pivot points to show the difference between the imagined farm and the actual farm. For example, after noting that each Iowa farmer supports 129 Americans, Pollan continues, "it can no longer support the four who live on it: The Naylor farm survives by the grace of Peggy Naylor's paycheck (she works for a social services agency in Jefferson) and an annual subsidy payment from Washington D.C." (34). It was as if Pollan had revealed a hidden world, completely unknown to nonrural people but vital to their very survival. The separation of urban and rural, to the detriment of the rural, is the structure against which students will need to learn to navigate if they are to shift their position from the margins to full participants in the public sphere, and for this project, in the academic classroom.

Next Steps

The purpose of this chapter has been to move from an initial question—"Why didn't my rural students want to share their expert knowledge in a college-level American literature survey course?"—to a possible answer and course of action for developing a critical rural pedagogy. From composition studies and literary theorists, I began with knowledge of critical pedagogy and how representations in texts reflect power structures. I discovered that traditional notions of critical pedagogy, though a useful starting place, were not sufficient when working with rural community college students. The basic structure of oppressor and oppressed, as defined by Freire, does not operate cleanly when the students who are marginalized, or oppressed, see themselves as members of the dominant culture, and therefore, not marginalized. At the same time, there are students of color and other marginalized groups in rural community colleges, and their struggle to minimize their rural connection because it is of lower status is complicated by their multiple layers of oppression, as defined by Freire. Further, my classroom presents a highly diverse situation, where individual students have differing amounts of wealth, resources, experiences beyond the community, and degree of connection to the rural community in which my campus is situated. This information provided me with a need to look more closely at how a critical rural pedagogy might be constructed, which will be discussed in Chapter 2. But let it suffice here to say that my conception of a critical rural pedagogy must take into account the multiple positions of power student occupy simultaneously, as well as the rich variation in students who are included in my definition of "rural students."

I also explored how the work of Donehower, Hogg, and Schell, who identified repeated uses of rural representation that foregrounded this geographic location and the people who inhabit it as lacking, lagging behind, or representatives of a rosy past, might be useful in this endeavor. In order to use these representations in the classroom, I needed to be sure they were repeated with their cultural and political implications with enough frequency that students can identify, recognize, and speak back against them. However, in order for a rural critical pedagogy to be useful at my community college, which has students from multiple locations and backgrounds, it needs to include techniques and topics that will benefit all students. With this in mind, I also included an examination of written texts from multiple genres to see if lack, lag, or rosy past representations appear consistently, frequently, and across time. Since these three representations do rise to that level, I can use them as topoi, through which all students can talk back critically against texts in American literature. Students with rural experiences can serve as experts, guides for the class, enriching inquiry into the construction and implications of representations of the rural when they appear in texts their American literature survey class covers. The power of the repeated, culturally dominant imagery negates the direct experiences of the people who live in rural spaces, explaining in part why my rural students silence themselves rather than identifying themselves as rural or experts in rural issues. Lack, lag, and rosy past have traction in historical and contemporary literature and public discourse. They are used uncritically and problematically in scholarly works, in government documents, and in multiple works of literature, memoirs, and popular texts.

In the next chapter, I will explore how others have approached these concerns. First, I will need to identify rural literacies and the extent to which they are defined and given room in the academic world to determine how they are foregrounded or buried in classrooms where rural students are present. Second, I will explore rural pedagogies, looking for use of those literary practices in academic settings as a way to foreground the development of specific pedagogies for my American literature survey courses.

Chapter Two

Using What They Know: Pedagogical Moves

In this chapter, I explore how to build a critical rural pedagogy that enables rural students to draw on their experiences and expertise as rural students, as I have tried to do specifically in my community college, and to engage American literature texts but with broader relevance. Ideally, this critical rural pedagogy will enable students to engage with the texts and bring their voices to the critiques as they develop and create richer, more complicated discussions of language and its use in these texts. It is my hope to show these students that they have an important contribution to make as participants in higher education. I also expect that a critical rural pedagogy would be useful to instructors and professors who are working with students in other rural community colleges. I am concerned that rural students are reluctant to use their rural expertise in my American literature survey course and in the world of higher education in general. Along with rural students' reticence to engage their expertise, I am concerned that most students oversimplify rural peoples and places and their relationships to other American citizens, and this leads to a flattening of their critical work in the American literature classroom. American literature texts that foreground rural people and places would seem a logical location for inserting means and structures to change this pattern.

As mentioned at the end of Chapter 1, I tentatively define rural literacies as specific knowledge built from living in rural spaces, including written skills, social understanding, and knowledge of places, which are central to living successfully in a rural environment. This is a problematic definition because it is built on a fluid understanding of what rural spaces are, but it will serve as a starting point. As discussed in Chapter 1, the rural is not consistently defined in public discourse; it is sometimes delimited by geography, or by population, or by the ways that it is "not urban." Additionally, the students who inhabit the rural space in my community college are not a homogenous set but reflect a range in ages, socioeconomic status, ethnicities, cultural backgrounds, and life experiences. For my students, rural literacies, and the extent to which their experiences are foregrounded or buried in academic classrooms, is important because I want to leverage their rural literacies to help connect them to the classroom and to their place in the larger world of higher education. In this chapter, I want to explore how rural literacies can be used strategically to enrich the teaching of American literature texts, especially when the term rural literacy is already highly contested. Rural students' literacy practices need to be part of a thoughtful construction of classroom activities and tasks. A critical rural pedagogy should include a set of classroom practices or guidelines that provide ways for students to enact their understandings of the rural world when they are examining texts. In my class, American literature, I need not only to be aware of rural literacy but also to call on students to use those practices. Later, I provide a brief overview of rural pedagogies in order to reveal the problems I hope to ameliorate for students in my American literature courses and other such classes taught in rural settings. Finally, I lay out the theoretical groundwork for a critical rural pedagogy that 1) aims to accept and problematize students' use of language around their rural experiences; 2) gives students an opportunity to develop tactics and skills for critical work that builds on their rural knowledge; and 3) contextualizes rural students as both within the dominant culture and marginalized. I plan to develop a critical pedagogy to deploy in the interrogation of texts by students in a rural classroom setting and empower these students to use their rural expertise as a critical focus when examining texts.

Vignette: The Silenced Student

In the fall of 2010, I was invited to present at the conference of the Washington Community College Humanities Association. This annual conference had been a part of my professional development for over a decade, and I felt familiar with the faculty who generally attended, usually eighty to a hundred two-year college professors from multiple disciplines in the humanities. In the past, my presentations typically focused on sharing best practices, collaborating with other faculty outside my discipline, and sharing conversations around our subjects, students, and pedagogy. So, I decided this conference would be an appropriate venue to test out concepts that undergird this book. Specifically, I wanted to discuss the unquestioned "normativity" of urban/suburban representations that then put the rural into the "abnormal" category, creating a perception for students from rural backgrounds of being outsiders in the academy. I also wanted to share Kim Donehower, Charlotte Hogg, and Eileen E. Schell's summary of the three major conceptions of the rural, as places of lack, lag, or the rosy past. I expected that this group, with its critical stance and knowledge of both community college classrooms and community college students, might make me aware of strengths and flaws as I developed my theoretical approaches to engaging rural students in American literature survey courses.

This audience should have been especially attuned to students similar to those at Centralia College. I wanted to determine whether my initial concerns about how rural students might silence themselves due to the dominant culture's marginalization were on track. I hoped that feedback from colleagues would help me create a more nuanced understanding of my concerns about how to develop more complex and complicated analyses of texts with my rural students. Other community college instructors seemed the most useful audience to help me begin developing a critical rural pedagogy that would operate more effectively with students who don't see themselves as marginalized but, I was more and more convinced, acted like people with less power and status in the academic world because of their geographically and culturally influenced experiences. Specifically, I hoped a more targeted pedagogy that foregrounds rural students' concerns might help me intervene to alter a perceived knowledge/

power imbalance and encourage students to bring their rural experiences into classroom discussion and textual analysis in myriad ways that they would find valuable and meaningful.

My presentation, titled "Lost in the Fields: Representations of the Rural in American Literature," was well attended, with fifteen community college faculty members in the room. Additionally, I was pleased to discover that because the conference started on a Friday and was held on the campus of Cascadia Community College, ten undergraduate students were also present. I believe they were enticed into attending with extra credit and a writing assignment by at least one of the Cascadia English faculty. My presentation began with the assertion that students who come to higher education from small towns and rural areas recognize established binaries. By the time I arrived at the third binary, "urban and suburban = well educated" (accompanied with photos of a university, students in a large library, graduation) versus "rural = not well educated" (one-room schoolhouse, Montezuma, Iowa, Future Farmers of America students in an antiquated gym with blue corduroy jackets on), I had noted one student seemed to be paying particular attention. The student leaned forward at his desk, nodding his head in agreement at particular moments.

Later, this student turned to look at each person talking during the question-and-answer period after the main presentation. The student also wore a plaid shirt, identical to those for sale at Tractor Supply, and a pair of Carhartt boots. I assumed that this student came from a rural, and perhaps actively agricultural, background. As the presentation wound down, one of the faculty attendees asked whether I had heard from rural students in response to my assertions, and, if so, what they had thought, and then turned directly to this student and asked, "What do rural students think?" To my horror and surprise, I witnessed exactly the othering and marginalization of a rural student about which I had been theorizing. The student's physical reaction was striking. He quickly leaned back in the chair, pulled in arms and legs close to the body, and looked down, then at other students, and finally up at me. The student did not look back at the professor who had posed the question. The student was silent. Calling attention to and labeling this student as rural had been enough to cause him to retreat.

This student's body language was identical to the response I had witnessed repeatedly when students from a visible minority group on campus had been asked to speak for an entire group in the past. An uncomfortable yet familiar moment was playing out yet again during my presentation. I was reminded, for example, that despite my past efforts at classroom management on my own small campus, I have witnessed a single Muslim student asked to speak for all Muslims, a student of color asked to speak for all students of color, a younger student asked to speak for all young students, an older adult student asked to speak for all adult students, and a veteran asked to speak for all veterans. In the past, though, these requests had come from other students, not from a teaching colleague who I assumed would be more sensitive to the consequences of asking any one person to represent a large group, especially a marginalized group. Before, I had been in my own classroom, with some degree of influence over next steps and classroom culture, but now, during the presentation, a professor, an authority figure, had clearly perceived the student as a representative of a foreign, exotic, outsider group. And, more surprisingly, the other faculty members in the presentation audience turned to look at the student as if he had been invisible to them until the person asking the question had "outed" him.

It appeared that my theorized concerns about rural students choosing to silence themselves were being blatantly enacted right in front of me as I witnessed this student positioned to represent a marginalized group, rural students. Despite rural students' desire to attach themselves to the dominant culture, clearly this student responded as a person without power, exactly the opposite of what I hope for my students. It is my desire to provide opportunities in the classroom that will help students recognize that they are important in the academic world and that their life experiences as rural students are valid and relevant in discussions of American literature—but

I want to do so in a manner that avoids the discomfort and alienation that the student described above experienced at my talk. I emerged from the conference with a renewed sense that I was on the right track in wanting to develop a more effective version of critical pedagogy, a version that takes into account the complicated hierarchy rural students do not willingly recognize but are subjected to, to empower my rural students in the classroom and perhaps to help build their confidence as people with important ideas to share in the academy. It appeared that students with rural life experiences have been overlooked. In the most extreme examples, rural students may have learned to make their backgrounds invisible in a college classroom.

Defining Rural Literacy

In their first book, *Rural Literacies* (2007), Donehower, Hogg, and Schell define those literacies as "the particular kinds of literate skills needed to achieve the goals of sustaining life in rural areas" (4). This definition only goes so far in clarifying the term. It is circular in its logic because it requires a clear understanding of the rural, which is also a highly contentious term. If we cannot agree on what constitutes the "rural," then how can we pinpoint the literate skills required to "sustain life" there? Because the rural is not a static concept, but rather a dynamic, variable, and contested reality composed of multiple, agonistic literacy practices, I begin our conversation with what I mean by the term "rural literacies." While I have much more to say throughout this section, suffice it to say here that I include three components in rural literacies: 1) special knowledge of a geographic location; 2) the use of reading and writing to establish a voice in a rural community; and 3) the ideals for reading and writing imposed on rural peoples by urban outsiders. I came to this brief definition through an examination of the current uses of the term *rural literacy*, which follows.

In order to develop a critical rural pedagogy, I begin by offering a brief overview of some ways that rural literacy has been defined. Rural literacy is important to my thinking about a critical rural pedagogy because defining and limiting the term *rural literacy* will help me to focus on the abilities and skills that students from rural backgrounds bring with them to the college classroom. Definitions like that offered by Donehower, Hogg, and Schell are not sufficient because they lack the connection between the rural and the rest of the world. Rural literacies are not lesser than general literacies. I prefer to structure rural literacy as additional knowledge and myriad skills that rural students bring with them to their academic careers. In terms of developing a critical rural pedagogy, only after I have distilled a clearer understanding of what literacy students bring with them can I move toward attempting to develop a pedagogy that brings these students' specific knowledge and experiences to the foreground in a college class where they need to operate across the multiple perspectives of rural literacy. There is not a single rural literacy. Instead, rural literacies cross boundaries and constantly shift, depending on geographic location and context.

Even a small overview of the ways scholars attempt to define rural literacy reveals the fault lines around this problematic term, so I will discuss five key and contested conceptions of rural literacy. In summary, the first sees rural literacy as a limited, specific set of academic, basic skills, learned by rote in elementary schools; the second posits rural literacy as the ability to "read" a rural space, not just in written text, but through visual clues that have meaning for people living in the rural space; the third sees rural literacy as a practice of a way of life, a deep knowledge of a specific location and the community that develops as a result of that shared knowledge; the fourth ties rural literacy to academic and economic reading and writing tasks that can be accomplished after learning from an educational entity, like a school or rural college; finally, the last argues against a general definition of rural literacy, claiming in direct opposition to the other definitions that there are multiple rural literacies and that each is determined by the individual tasks using reading/writing that are valued and regularly engaged in by a rural subgroup, for example the Amish. As I read the work of these scholars, I found my own thinking on the subject paralleled much of these scholars' work except for the first example, which reduces literacy to basic skills and rote memorization. Even in my overview, it is clear that there is not an absolute consensus for the content, structure, purpose, or object of the term *rural literacy*.

That said, let me briefly distill the core elements in my own definition of rural literacy. First, rural literacy, writ large, is a special knowledge of a particular geographical location and how to successfully operate linguistically in that space; second, rural literacy is learning to use reading and writing to establish oneself as a voice in a rural community and against discourses of the rural that circulate inside that community; and third, rural literacy is a set of ideals for reading and writing that has been imposed on the rural community by urban outsiders in order to control the rural for the urban's purposes. Rural literacy can be defined or identified in multiple tasks, skills, and points of view, and is continuously changing to meet the needs and situations of rural peoples in various locations. But now let's look at others' conceptions more closely.

The first approach to rural literacy, and one that runs counter to my developing definition, appears in an early study that defines rural literacy as K–12 teachers' in-class methodology. In this sense, rural literacy is understood narrowly as basic skills in reading and writing that are taught in school settings using primarily rote memorization. In the late 1980s, Anthony Petrosky studied literacy practices in rural Mississippi Delta public schools, and his observations suggest that students' uniform responses based on rote memorization (65) formed the basis of a basic skills curriculum in literacy. Mississippi Delta students were perceived to be lacking in the most elemental of literacy skills, so the teachers used pedagogy "grounded in rote learning, as opposed, say, to notions of learning as generative" (65). Rural literacy, as reported by Petrosky, involves top-down educational policies and reforms intended to be implemented in the public school system, and through that gateway, filtered out into the larger community. These policies are couched in the language of reform.

Rural literacies, in this case, are a prescribed set of tasks, skills, or specific pieces of information that rural public-school students are lacking, identified by state-level curriculum developed outside the local community. Rural literacy, as defined with this deficiency model, lists skills, abilities, and knowledges students do not have and then fills the vacuum of what is missing. This form of rural literacy does not build toward any sort of critical pedagogy. In fact, it is in direct opposition to the ideas of empowering marginalized students. Instead, it is a method of control by a bureaucratic system that allows only for the most minimal system of tracking, with progress a measurement of a student's ability to memorize prescribed ideas and skills. This form of rural literacy does not provide insights that can inform the critical rural pedagogy I hope to develop. Instead, it reinforces the constructed representation of rural children as lacking in something that must be provided by outsiders, and it suggests that rural children are not necessarily capable of higher-order critical work, as such work is explicitly excluded from the school curriculum.

Petrosky's study focuses on two majority–African American public schools. The intersection of race and educational history in Mississippi are undercurrents of his work, as he identifies percentages of students of color and education levels of the larger community in racial terms. However, his results include a caution against curricular ordering of basic skills with writing first and then more advanced skills later. He also warns against attempts to generalize his findings beyond the classrooms he has studied. He calls for careful examination of mandates from beyond the classroom and district because they removed teachers from the development of policy and programs (71). Throughout his assertions, Petrosky's study conflates literacy with curriculum and pedagogy. Additionally, while his work is valuable, his definition of rural literacy does not match that of the other four scholars I include in this discussion: Jacqueline Edmondson, Jean-Paul Hautecoeur, Katherine Kelleher Sohn, and Andrea Fishman. Petrosky's discussion is also of limited use for my project, other than as a reminder that rural literacy has been used as a limiting construct intended to "fix" broken students. My students, certainly, are familiar with this attitude in the No Child Left Behind legislation and standardized tests.

The second approach to defining rural literacy is presented by Jacqueline Edmondson, an academic working in a rural Minnesota town, which she names Prairie Town, who distinguishes "traditional rural literacies" (66) from other literacies by noting that they are a complicated set of required structures used to interpret and access the people, organizations, and landforms of rural spaces. I agree with her insight that life in a rural place has its own complications that are not obvious to the casual observer. Just as with other cultural constructions people use to navigate lives intertwined with others, rural literacies include information and skills beyond traditional definitions of general literacy. She defines rural literacy as a way for rural people to respond to "agrarian republicanism, socialism, and early American capitalism" by "reading farm and land" (51), "reading community" (53), and "reading school" (59). She also suggests that rural literacy serves to change the urban-centered conversation about the rural because rural people control the conversation. She suggests that rural people redefine how they are perceived by others when they act by "reading the 'rural problem'" and renaming it "the country life movement" (63). Despite her claim of agency, I have to question her conclusion here. She suggests that rural literacy includes controlling the imagery and representations used by nonrural people, but she does not adequately support her assertion. The language of a "rural problem" is still endemic in the larger culture, despite efforts by rural people to control that language. Instead, this highlights the marginalized position of rural people. They are not in a position of power; they cannot guide the conversation about themselves beyond their own communities.

For Edmondson, rural literacy focuses on an object, system, or idea that is to be understood, which is in opposition to Petrosky's discrete writing/reading skills-based definition. She uses the term "reading" to describe a variety of structures, including both written and oral forms, through which people living in rural areas develop their understanding of their experiences in a specific geographic location. A familiarity with peoples' past in specific geographic locations underlies her definition of rural literacy. This connection to place is central, and all the specific ways she identifies to "read" the situations and needs of people in this location becomes the basis for literacy. Using Edmondson's lens, rural literacy then is malleable, varying from location to location. There may be general similarities in rural literacy that focus on agriculture, or cultural contexts and structures, but the specific skills and knowledge to interpret important information from written documents, oral traditions, and visual cues in the landscape will be different in each rural location.

Rural literacy, as Edmondson defines it, would also change over time as the needs of people and changes to the land and its uses adjust with and against relationships with entities and agencies in the larger world. I appreciate the flexibility of Edmondson's conception. As she has outlined them, literacy skills are situational, embedded in the culture, geographies, and ways of knowing and doing that are specific to various places and times. She also suggests that rural literacies are often tied to a location so that any person who wishes to use this knowledge is also limited in some applications of these literacies. Her ideas crystallize in some small way rural students' need to master the ability to work in multiple contexts at the same time, shifting their language use as they move between locations and situations. This flexibility and connection to appropriate audience has been well documented in other students who navigate through multiple worlds concurrently, for example, when people code switch.

Students' ability to alter their language is also made visible in Juan Guerra's work with disenfranchised students who need to make use of *modalities of memory* to "negotiate the challenges they face in Life in the Neither/Nor" (2). Although my students operate across multiple, often concurrent positions of power, I agree with Guerra that there are ways my students may work across the third space, literacy shifts students make across spaces, both physical and cultural (4). Another scholar who is working to clarify the shifts individuals made when working across linguistics spaces, A. Suresh Canagarajah, uses the term *translingual* to capture a similar move students make when operating in multiple language spaces. Canagarajah uses the term to describe the "ability to merge different language resources in situated interactions for new meaning construction" (1–2). More complicated than code switching, Canagarajah is suggesting that when interacting with texts across locations, the students' actions are "hybridizing and emergent, facilitating creative tensions between languages" (2), and he calls explicitly for making a classroom "a safe house" for "developing relevant strategies and dispositions for translingual literacies in the contact zones outside the classroom" (9).

Edmondson, Guerra, and Canagarajah all present clarifying descriptions of language use that I have noticed in my classroom and community. As I have observed rural students making these linguistic and cultural moves in multiple locations—for example, the same student will draw from different vocabulary and language patterns in my classroom, at the county fair, and in their place of worship—I generally agree with Edmondson's conception of situational literacy skills, and I am encouraged by Guerra's and Canagarajah's recent scholarship that also calls for classroom practices to support students as they work across literacy locations. I can develop class activities that allow students to explore the ways they maneuver through variations of rural literacies, and then, how this might or might not play out in the American literature they are studying.

The third conception of rural literacy focuses on a practice of a way of life, a deep knowledge of a specific location and the community that develops as a result of that shared knowledge. For example, Jean-Paul Hautecoeur defines and identifies rural literacies in a way that accounts for the expertise and resources present for people living in rural contexts. He focuses on the cultural basis for rural literacy. He opens with an idea from Jean Bruno, who has written about the decline of agriculture in Canada for the Canadian Agriculture Federation, which Hautecoeur describes as a "positive view," defining

> the rural space as a particular use of space and social life . . . . More than a distinct bio-physical environment, the contemporary rurality presents three specific attributes. First, a human, ecological, cultural and historical patrimony of high value, which is also a certain way of life. Second, an intimate knowledge of the land, the territory, which creates an identity. Lastly, a strong community spirit or solidarity which builds a society of mutual knowledge. (18–19)

Bruno notes three overlapping sources for rural literacies: patrimony, land, and community, and he argues that each must be central to defining rural literacies. Interestingly, in defining rural literacy, he parallels the three rural topoi (lack, lag, and rosy past) that I discussed in Chapter 1, which was surprising since Hautecoeur suggests that Bruno's conception of rural literacy reflects a positive or value to overall literacy that is added to the skill sets of rural people.

From this perspective, Hautecoeur builds an "action research perspective," which highlights local people's ways of posing "questions of shortfall, development, cultural change, preservation and revitalization of cultural heritage[, . . . and] 'illiteracy'" and suggests attention to "specialized terms of individuals' linguistic competence" and "plans to resist the destructuring of their community" (9). He does not recognize the negative references to lack, lag, and rosy past in his own work. I believe this is another example of how these representations have become so deeply embedded in the general culture that they go unquestioned and repeated, even by Hautecoeur. He does point out a difficulty, however, when he argues that current rural literacy practices are a source not only of tension but also of domination and control of rural peoples by urban outsiders.

I agree with his concerns about hegemony here, and he has clearly identified the power imbalance created by those outside of the rural who use and control the rural for reasons that do not include the needs of its people. Hautecoeur provides a turn that is useful in developing a critical rural pedagogy that accounts for context and specific actions for students to use when working against these stereotypes. Hautecoeur advocates developing rural literacy practices at the local level, by those who need and use them, which then separates those practices from the systems of measurement placed on them by outside agents. Following his lead, I hope to find ways for my rural students to use their local knowledge of agricultural practices, specific locations, and social interactions as points of comparison against which literary pieces may be examined. For Hautecoeur, rural literacy is the battleground for controlling definitions and terms of rural literacy, as well as for how these ideas may be deployed.

Hautecoeur provides me with a framework to more deeply examine the dominance of outside forces on rural people's representations in texts. The power differential he describes fits the framework of critical pedagogy, at least roughly, because it situates the urban/suburban author and publisher in the power position with rural peoples clearly marginalized, subjugated by the language used to describe and control them. Hautecoeur's structure encourages me to provide activities and discussion spaces in the classroom that may draw rural students into a clearer understanding of their less-powerful position in this structure. However, as I discussed earlier, rural students occupy more than one position in the power structure. Hautecoeur's conception does not include the possibility that rural students may not be marginalized in all ways. Despite my deep concern about his limited perspective, his work does suggest an opening for more critical examination of American literature, with the students' rural literacy providing the expertise for a more complicated deconstruction of those texts. I can ask students to orient themselves within the constructions and discourses on the rural, allowing them to better understand how language represents and creates realities, and to what end for themselves, their families, and others. I am also further convinced of the malleable and contested space within the term rural literacy. While I am often in agreement with Edmondson and Hautecoeur, and their conceptions have areas of overlap, they are not identical.

The fourth conception of rural literacy I am considering here defines the term through academic and economic reading and writing tasks that can be accomplished after students have attended a rural college. Katherine Kelleher Sohn, in her influential text *Whistlin' and Crowin' Women of Appalachia: Literacy Practices since College* (2006), states that the context for rural literacy includes primarily actions that are explicitly enacted through reading and writing in college. In her book, she follows female students through their college experiences and beyond. Academic reading and writing are by default the context of rural literacy for these Appalachian women. Sohn's second chapter "reveals how the women moved from silence to voice to identity by maintaining their dialect throughout college and beyond, by discovering the power of expressivist writing and completing their degrees to enhance their identity as strong women of Appalachia, by gaining economic and social power, and by remaining in their communities" (5). Her concept directly opposes that of Petrosky in that his rural literacy required abandoning rural speech patterns for more "correct" patterns of Standard English language use. Sohn disagrees. For her students, maintaining their Appalachian speech patterns in written work is necessary for building a literate identity that is both strong and tied to their geographic location. For Sohn, literacy is closely tied to academic tasks and economic advancement through a college degree but also to empowerment, defined as women developing and then using their voices in their current communities. Asserting one's identity comes from using reading and writing to explore, develop, and reinforce that identity.

Rural literacy, as defined by Sohn, is then the act of reading and writing and the asserting of personhood through these tasks. Literacy is explicitly intended to help people find and express themselves. Literacy is a tool through which individuals, who happen to be in Appalachia, enlarge their sense of self and empower their own actions. Her conception of literacy has direct implications for my possible classroom work. For her, it is the act of reading and writing in the classroom, while maintaining a respect for the linguistic patterns that reflect students' identities and nurture the use of voice, that empowers students from Appalachia, and, at least conceptually, should also serve my rural students in Centralia. However, there is a hitch. I am directed to teach and evaluate student writing against Standard English practices. While I might encourage students to use nonstandard dialects when working on informal responses, when participating in class discussion and when developing drafts of longer works, formal essays are to be evaluated against a student's ability to operate in Standard English. As noted previously, rural students are already proficient at code switching for a community and an academic audience. I have not resolved this tension, but it is important to acknowledge that when students switch from their local dialects to Standard English, this is another moment in which to examine the ways that language choice and use alters the reality of what is developed in text.

While noble, Sohn's definition, again, does not exactly match Donehower, Hogg, and Schell's definition, Edmondson's ways to read rural communities, Hautecoeur's tension between practice and outsiders, or Petrosky's elevation of rote memorization for mastering basic reading and writing skills to fill in missing abilities. However, Sohn does further illustrate the multilayered uses of the term *literacy*, let alone *rural literacy*. Context, how rural literacy is situated in everyday life, matters, as it does for

Donehower and her colleagues, for Edmonson, for Hautecoeur, and, increasingly, for me.

The fifth conception of rural literacy is drawn from Andrea Fishman's ethnographic study of Amish reading and writing patterns, *Amish Literacy: What and How it Means* (1988), in which she states that rural literacy is determined by the individual reading/writing tasks that are valued and used regularly by this rural subgroup. Fishman asserts that a general statement of rural literacy is inadequate. She asserts that there is no one "monolithic condition or decontextualized set of discrete skills transferrable across all contexts" for a singular rural literacy (133), which is in concert with Edmondson, Donehower et al., and Hautecoeur. She argues for a definition of literacy that is not universal, not static. Amish literacy, a subset of rural literacy, fits the needs and cultural requirements of the Amish; "they are sufficiently observant and aware to discern and adopt those practices that will best serve their own way of life" (133). Her work suggests that it is important for me to determine what rural western Washington literacy might be, or, more important, that a specific form of rural literacy that operates in and around Centralia should be explored by my students. Fishman identifies six types of reading that "count": 1) "the ability to discriminate among print materials; to find the desired portion" of a text; 2) "following written directions"; 3) "the ability to recall"; 4) memorization; 5) "the ability to synthesize what is read in a single text into what is already known or to synthesize information across texts in an organized whole"; and 6) "to empathize with characters in a text" (134–37).

As for writing, Fishman "found . . . the abilities to copy, to encode, to list, to follow format and to choose content" (137) central in importance in Amish literacy. In addition to her analysis and identification of specific literacy skills and abilities prized by the Amish, Fishman adamantly argues against the back-to-basics movement, which focuses on rote memorization of isolated facts, stating that "just as the back-to-basics zealots might be wise to stop and define basics and decide which basics should be returned to by whom, so the literacy evangelists might be wise to stop crusading for reading and writing long enough to decide what those words mean to the people they consider the unconverted"

(141). Fishman's theorizing of Amish literacy is different from the other conception in that she subdivides rural literacy into multiple rural literacies, using the Amish as a primary example. This is certainly useful for me and my students as an example of working against cultural representations of a simplified, uncomplicated rural. Fishman is advocating for multiple rural literacies based on the existence of multiple groups within the rural environment. Hautecoeur would concur, as he also advocates for a definition of rural literacy that is tied to specific locations.

Even with this brief overview, it is clear that there is not an absolute consensus for the content, structure, purpose, or object of the term *rural literacy*. As a result, as I stated earlier, my own definition of rural literacy includes three points, which I repeat here. First, rural literacy, writ large, is a special knowledge of a particular geographical location and how to successfully operate linguistically in that space; second, rural literacy is learning to use reading and writing to establish oneself as a voice in a rural community and against discourses of the rural that circulate inside that community; and, third, rural literacy is a set of ideals for reading and writing that has been imposed on the rural community by urban outsiders in order to control the rural for the urban's purposes. Rural literacy can be defined or identified in multiple tasks, skills, and points of view, and is continuously changing to meet the needs and situations of rural peoples in various locations.

This definition may serve as the basis for resistance and for a critical rural pedagogy that will allow students to enact a richer response to texts. The literacy practices students bring with them to my rural community college should be part of a thoughtful construction of classroom activities and tasks. As I pointed out at the start of this chapter, a critical rural pedagogy, a set of classroom practices that provide ways for students to enact their understandings of the rural world when they are examining texts—and specifically in my class, American literature—needs not only to be aware of rural literacy but also to call on students to use those practices. In the remainder of this book, I will explore these threads and determine how to use them in order to empower rural students in college American literature classes. Ultimately, I hope to engage these students in critical conversations that have meaning for them and to help them recognize the importance of their presence in and contribution to the college environment.

Toward a Pedagogy That Uses Rural Literacies

Problems and Inconsistencies with Current Rural Pedagogies

Given the range of antagonistic/competing definitions of rural literacy, it is not surprising that there is also no consensus on what a rural pedagogy might be, nor did I discover any clear guidance in developing a pedagogy for rural students enrolled in a survey-level American literature course at a small community college. Just as no definition of rural literacy has universally consistent purchase in the field, neither does any concept of rural pedagogy. In some ways, the term is even more problematic than rural literacy. My review of rural pedagogies reveals that there are variable and contested ways of conceiving the aims and practices of rural pedagogy. The core tensions represented by these approaches tend to oversimplify the rural, homogenize the rural, or merely provide a means for the author to posture, generally around the political perspectives that underlie pedagogy. There is also a tension between idiosyncratic curricula based on very local knowledges and top-down preset curricula rooted in broader national learning outcomes that are created outside of and then imposed upon rural locations. On the one hand, while having a set curriculum stabilizes what a rural pedagogy might look like, the tendency to homogenize the rural can flatten out the ability of such pedagogy to respond to students' experiences. On the other hand, pedagogies that are wholly situational risk diffusing the model of rural pedagogy so much that it ceases to recognizably exist.

Just as with the concept of rural literacy, I advocate a rural pedagogy that draws on situational, geographically bounded, place-specific sets of reading and writing skills. I argue that rural pedagogy needs to provide a means for incorporating the specific location in which students are working by using a variation of critical pedagogy that attempts to work with the need for students to identify with the dominant culture while concurrently occupying a position of marginalization, which they may not be willing to recognize. What follows attempts to clarify the wide-ranging uses of the term *rural pedagogy*. And, specifically, I will define rural pedagogy in terms of a critical project that aims to empower rural students who take my American literature survey courses through the use of a critical rural pedagogy. Ideally, these ideas should be useful for other instructors who are also working in similarly rural community colleges. By the end of this chapter, I will develop a set of guiding principles that are at the heart of a critical rural pedagogy that could be used not only in my classes but also in other rural community colleges. It is important for me to identify how and when power influences curricular choices, as well as what the content and consequences of controlling terms are for people in rural contexts. For this reason, facilitating students' experiences so that they take a closer look at the use of language to control and define rural people and places is one of my goals. Ideally, students can then learn to deploy techniques, such as the topoi of lack, lag, or rosy past, strategically for their own purposes through a critical rural pedagogy.

My overview of the term *rural pedagogy* reveals at least two strands. The first is that pedagogical discussions around the rural focus almost exclusively on students in kindergarten through twelfth grade. Despite the focus on younger students, I hoped to find pedagogical techniques, strategies, or theories that use students' experiences as the basis for building knowledge and skills that could transfer into or inform working with students at the college level. Then students may be better prepared for using their expertise as a basis for critical interrogation of representations of the rural they will encounter in higher education. As this next section will illustrate, these resources are of unfortunately limited value in developing a pedagogy that is explicitly critical in its stance.

The second strand is the fragmented use and understanding of the term *rural pedagogy*. I have classified the examples I will share as "inconsistent rural pedagogies." The commonality in these pedagogies is that they exist solely because of the rural place where students are being taught. They seem almost "accidental" pedagogies, something developed on the fly because of pressures from state boards of education and the need to control curriculum or because of threats to consolidate small school districts. Pedagogical discussions are then further split into isolated conversations about the content of curriculum or classroom practices. As an overview, these pedagogies call for using rural K–12 schools 1) to fulfill a personal agenda for a utopian sense of community; 2) to create a local food and resources movement; 3) to promote an "American rural way of life" (Haas and Nachtigal vi); 4) to expand curriculum to include local geography and history; and finally, 5) to advocate for small schools with individualized attention, perhaps even "model classrooms which use instructional management" systems (Gjelten, "Elk River" 218).

I will provide an overview of the conversations to demonstrate the general tone and to identify small moments that have helped me recognize the need to create a critical rural pedagogy that allows and encourages students to bring the range of their experiences into the academic space. Student should then be given classroom experiences that help them to develop tactics and skills for exploring what these experiences mean in relation to content materials, in this case, representations of the rural and the constructed worlds they are reading about in American literature. This critical rural pedagogy should address questions of power and hierarchy that are embedded in American literature and serve as a starting point for students to further discuss and dissect the ramifications of these constructed representations. The classroom will then serve as a location for helping students develop their ability to speak back, to respond to the ways these constructions of power and representation influence their lives, and to decide how they might respond. At the same time, a critical rural pedagogy is still required to account for students' abilities in regard to state standards and national benchmarks. For my students, their coursework needs to demonstrate skills, abilities, and knowledge in order to earn college-level credit at my community college and to be transferable to other colleges and universities.

Inconsistent and K–12 Dominance of Rural Pedagogy

Paul Theobald, in his text *Teaching the Commons: Place, Pride, and the Renewal of Community* (1997), provides an example of the dominance of K–12 pedagogy. His book is less about curriculum and more about using rural schools, specifically kindergarten through twelfth grade public schools, to advance his personal vision of community. He generalizes all rural spaces into one homogenous context and makes a strategic choice to use small-town and rural schools as a first step to remaking America according to his "educational agenda" (120). He asserts that his agenda "has the best chance of catching on in rural America, where size is still manageable and where lingering vestiges of a sense of community yet remain" (120). This last statement especially suggests that he sees the rural through a sense of the rosy past. Rural schools are not necessarily smaller than their urban counterparts, thanks to the move to consolidate small districts, which has been in play since at least the early 1980s. There is also an uncomfortable sense that urban spaces have lost all community, which I would also dispute, or that rural classrooms somehow are more communal, which is also not always the case. Theobald flattens all communities into the idealized vision he is advocating at the expense of communities that already exist.

Theobald states that the curriculum in rural schools must be based in the local geography and issues. This would allow rural educators to become the agents of change who would use their classrooms and their work "as a moral endeavor to rebuild community," by which he means creating an anti-big business, anti-commodities-driven society (122). He calls his curriculum a "revitalization project" (124) that rebuilds community (122). His biased vision of rural communities as places that are broken or damaged in important ways is clear. I would dispute this understanding of the rural, instead noting that Theobald's work places him squarely in the cultural understanding of the rural as a place of lack and lag because they have lost a fictional version of community that Theobald espouses. Another problem is that he chooses rural pedagogy because he asserts that the size of the communities is manageable (120), an overgeneralization with which I strongly disagree. Given the complicated nature of defining a rural community, as discussed in the introduction to this project, his glib statement demonstrates his minimization of rural communities. He also equates a smaller number of people, again, a generalized statement, with an easier task for managers of schools who want to manipulate the learning environment.

Clearly, his focus is on the local school's classrooms, though his discussion suggests a lack of practical knowledge of rural schools. He does not address consolidation issues that move secondary classrooms a great distance from students' homes, and he repeatedly assumes that the old system of desks in rows and teachers talking while students take notes is still the norm (140). Even in 1997, when his book was published, rural teachers were using more varied pedagogies than Theobald asserts. Anecdotally, my own experiences as a high school English teacher in Iowa in the 1980s include entire rural districts with professional development that encouraged and required student-centered pedagogy, e.g., writing in multiple genres, student-developed projects, speeches, songs, use of popular culture images to make connections, student-led discussion, and nearly ubiquitous group work. Desks rarely stayed in rows.

Theobald's examples of an elementary teacher and a secondary teacher in rural schools illustrate his assertion that "explorations of subject matter" are "a matter of inquiry. Answers should not be provided by the teacher or the textbook. Rather they should be deliberated on and thereby constructed by the students" (139–40). While he seems to be advocating for pedagogy that might be critical, he does not say so explicitly. Because he calls for using the rural public school, a move that is clearly that of a dominating power over the less important or powerful rural educators and community, I have great concerns about whether a critical pedagogy is within his conceptualization. He is not advocating for a student-led curriculum so much as for a curriculum that encourages student involvement only to the extent that those students arrive at the vision of community he desires, a community that rejects big-business models.

The implications of Theobald's ideas for rural pedagogy become even more distant from the experiences of rural students and teachers when he extends his ideas into the preparation of teachers for rural schools. Theobald posits that new teachers in K–12 will best develop their vision of rural pedagogy when they attend rural universities. However, he is vague about what constitutes a rural university. Is it a state university located at a distance from urban centers—for example, a land-grant university such as Washington State University or Iowa State University? Is a rural university an institution that serves only or predominantly rural students? My concerns that Theobald is using rural pedagogy as a means for controlling a version of the rural that is not connected to the reality of rural life is only increased when he provides an example of an elementary teacher to solidify his perspective:

> [B]ecause he attended a rural university where professors were serious about preparing teachers for rural schools, he has latched onto and become committed to certain principles. The first is that he believes knowledge is socially constructed and that his instructional practices, therefore, must include socializing his students into the habit of courteous conversation and deliberation. He will not function as the provider of answers; he will, rather, facilitate the sound construction of answers by his students. (141)

Theobald continues to describe this new teacher more in terms of a noble calling (141) than of reinforcing marketplace or economic needs of the urban. It was unclear to me whether Theobald did not see or chose to ignore this concern. Instead, Theobald asserts that the new young male teacher will "do what he can to help his students visualize and then attend to the needs of the community of which they are a part. The students' place on earth, in fact, will be central to all of his curricular and instructional efforts" (141). In the era of No Child Left Behind legislation, this is not possible, and even in the late 1990s, for a first-year teacher to create a curriculum completely separate from state-level standards would have been a herculean task. Simply attending a rural university would not prepare a new teacher to work through the political concerns that underlie the curricular discussions at the district, school, or classroom level.

Theobald assumes that the professors at a rural university have a greater understanding of teaching in rural schools than professors in teacher education programs in general, which seems unlikely, especially in light of Eric Zencey's work (1996) pointing out a cultural disconnect between instructors who have limited experiences in rural places and their rural students. He writes one of the few essays about rural pedagogy by someone located in higher education, and he contrasts students who have a sense of place with "rootless professors" (16), pointing out that although most students attend university in their home states, their professors are often "cosmopoles . . . a class of transient exotics" (16). He further criticizes unrooted instructors who tend to mistake "disconnected from locale" for "educated" (16) and do not place value in "connectedness to place" (17), thereby diminishing the value of their students' prior knowledge. If Zencey's analysis is correct, the professors at a rural university, however it may be defined, do not have a specialized knowledge of the rural classrooms in which they are preparing students to teach after completing the teacher education program. In fact, these professors may be unprepared to conceptualize students' knowledge and experiences or the locations where their students will be teaching. Theobald's assertion that education students who attend rural universities are better prepared for the needs of students in a rural elementary classroom does not stand if Zencey is correct.

The concerns voiced by Zencey have been echoed by Valerie Mulholland in her 2012 article, "For All Students in This Place." She does not identify the professoriat who develop teacher education programs as especially capable of working with marginalized students because current teacher education programs work from a position of embedded white privilege. Instead, she advocates for a change in preservice teacher training to include "several years of systematic reflexive practice" so that young, mostly white, and mostly privileged teachers recognize their white privilege against the educational work of continued colonization of First Peoples in Canada. This is a direct response to Donehower, Hogg, and Schell's identification of lack, lag, and rosy past (190). Mulholland recognizes her own faulty lens when working with preservice teachers. She states, "What I failed to realize when I began this process was that until I incorporated antiracist theory and practices, my classes would be susceptible to a romantic view of the past that reified entrenched white-settler identities" (196).

As a professor in a teacher education program, Mulholland did not have a special sensitivity to one subgroup in her rural school. She came to an understanding of her white privilege only after years working in the classroom and training others to teach in K–12. White privilege and concerns about minority groups are difficult enough to negotiate when the culture at least speaks nominally about a gap or difference. Because rural students as a group are not discussed as an outsider group, realizing culturally influenced bias is equally, if not more, difficult for professors. Theobald's assertion that professors in a rural university would have special understandings of rural students is weakened by both Mulholland's and Zencey's work, which are based in more academically sound theories and support. Mulholland has struck an important idea. When working with rural students, who may be marginalized in some ways but may or may not be aware that they occupy a less powerful position, there is also a need for "systematic reflexive practice," to use her terms, for students.

I am also compelled to interject that rural students are not homogenously white. There are nuances of working against a multilayered identity—wanting to present as urban or suburban while also contending with either a connection to the white power structure or additionally as a student of color/marginalized person carrying that double weight of white power structures.

As I noted in the opening of this section, an investigation of pedagogy reveals educators' inconsistent approaches to working with rural students. Most of the discussion is dominated by work with K–12 schools. But moving on, there is a greater fracturing of the conversation along approaches to pedagogy in terms of curriculum. Clearly, there is not a point of connection, let alone consensus, for all the repeated uses of the term *rural pedagogy*.

Curriculum

Another way rural pedagogy is defined is by curricular content. It is important to note that the term *pedagogy* is often used interchangeably with curriculum, which I find particularly problematic. Pedagogy is the classroom practices and constructions for helping students to learn, to interact with new materials or ideas, and to improve specific skills. Curriculum is not the same. Instead, curriculum is the content of a course or discipline. Conflating these two terms creates confusion. Not surprisingly, exactly what students from rural places should learn is a heavily contested and political matter. Next, I will explore in more detail examples of pedagogies that call for using rural schools 1) to create a local food and resources movement; 2) to promote an "American rural way of life" (Haas and Nachtigal vi); and 3) to expand curriculum to include local geography and history. As I detail below, what I have found is that rural students tend to be exposed to inconsistent curricular content, some of which attempts to foreground the rural experience, and from this I taken away a realization that curricular control is often a locus for control of how the rural is envisioned and operates. This insight is central to my rural pedagogy because I hope to develop a critical rural pedagogy that questions where and how representations and control of the rural are visible in language. A pedagogy that has empowerment of students as one of its goals has some overlap with, but is not equivalent to, the rural pedagogies discussed below.

The first answer I will consider to the question "What is rural curriculum?" is presented by David W. Orr, a professor of environmental studies. He states that there will come a point at which the migration to urban and suburban spaces will be replaced with a move back to rural areas (227–28). He coins a new term when he states that "re-ruralization, in contrast, will require a curriculum that honors tradition, locality, rootedness, ecological competence, and the attributes that hold people and land together in harmony" (231). As others have done, Orr articulates a false sense that rural people stay in one specific location. He seems unaware that there is movement between rural locations, and today, in the era of the interstate highway, lots of driving between rural and more populous spaces, perhaps even daily.

Orr advocates for this change from the only curriculum currently in use, the "urban curriculum" that educates students to be "urban with urban appetites, skills, minds, dependencies, and expectations" (228). Although he is not clear just what these appetites, etc., might be, his overall point reinforces my concerns that rural students have been required to follow a curriculum developed by an outside group, generally a state education department that must also now consider the national common core and state mandates. Certainly, a critical pedagogy would seem to be useful in helping students push back against this dominating force.

Orr then goes on to call for more agriculturally based education embedded in the liberal arts across the curriculum. His list of what rural students need to know how to do includes: grow enough food on local farms and in gardens to feed the population, generate energy from renewable sources, substitute local goods for imports, keep investment capital in the community and grow that capital, purify "without chemicals, eliminate toxic wastes and restore degraded environments," raise children who will work hard and, finally, be good citizens/neighbors (228). Orr's call is an incarnation of a familiar desire to change the content of curriculum in rural schools that is repeated by numerous others. Agricultural knowledge figures prominently in the "new" curriculum, and each proponent adds their own interests to the mix, for example: environmental concerns, religious doctrine, or economic independence. There is a concerning repeat of Theobald's impulse to control the curriculum again here. The environmental and sustainability threads in Orr's curriculum may or may not develop out of a critical pedagogy, let alone one that attempts to empower rural students. Orr is attempting to control the outcomes of the curriculum for his own purposes rather than the organically derived curricular outcomes that students from rural areas might develop. There is an impulse in Orr's writing to create a small, subsistence form of farming, more akin to the ideals of the rosy past than the current economic needs of rural agriculture.

Despite Orr's and others' calls, there has not been a corresponding response to remake the overall curriculum in rural schools. There is a program in rural high schools for students to improve their skills and knowledge of local agriculture, Future Farmers of America, known more often by its initials FFA. But there has not been a corresponding program in public schools for younger children. Additionally, the current limitations created by the federal mandates of No Child Left Behind (NCLB) work against agriculturally based curricula, focusing instead on concepts and means of measuring progress that are embedded in an urban or suburban experience. Recently, the rise of the Common Core State Standards, which are national in their stance and therefore not connected to local and regional literacies, adds to the pressure on rural schools to conform, reducing the likelihood that Orr's vision can be enacted on a large scale.

A second approach to rural pedagogy that promotes an "American rural way of life" as curriculum is also foregrounded in Toni Haas and Paul Nachtigal's brief collection of essays on "good literature on rural lifeways, environments, and purposes of education" (vi). Haas and Nachtigal reinforce the idea that there is an "American rural way of life" (vi) that gives priority to "deeper bonds with family, friends, and the world around them" (vi) rather than material gain. Unfortunately, their statement reveals a tendency to project a rosy past onto the rural rather than a clear-eyed understanding of rural places and people. There is also a clear statement that the rural environment is lacking, hence the need to use public schools in the service of "protecting self-determination" (vi). Schools then are necessary for "equipping rural students and the adults who surround them with tools to create a different, better future" (vi). My concern here is that Haas and Nachtigal do not recognize value in the rural as it exists. Instead, in a move that is reminiscent of the colonizing gaze described by Mary Louise Pratt, they minimize what exists in order to build a new version of the rural that matches their ideals. They place themselves above the students and communities they purport to improve in an obvious power hierarchy. Additionally, they again focus exclusively on K–12 students, and there is little in their overall approach that is helpful for me when working with undergraduates.

Haas and Nachtigal disavow the use of a national curriculum and instead advocate for a curriculum that focuses on local geographic spaces. Through in-depth study of the local, students engage in a "careful study of one's own habitat [that] reveals truth about the entire planet" (2). This curriculum should then be combined with entrepreneurial education in concert with "state and local development agencies, extension agents, and community colleges" (16). Students would be engaged in a pedagogy that overtly draws on the idea that they will stay in their rural communities and not be required to leave the area for an education or to find fulfilling and economically feasible work.

As I envision the practical use of Haas and Nachtigal's call, for example, such a curriculum might focus on locally relevant sources of revenue: forestry practices in the Pacific Northwest or in the Midwest, agricultural practices that deviate from monoculture so that risk is mitigated by multiple crops. Despite Haas and Nachtigal's naiveté, I believe it should be possible to enhance pedagogical approaches to American literature in the college classroom by tapping into this call for local, place-based practical knowledge. Rural students' practical knowledge and skills can then serve as a jumping-off point for richer interpretations of text and discussions with classmates, as well as for application of critical reading and writing skills to their own lives. The context in which this use of local knowledge is called into the classroom would need careful development, however. In order not to replicate these authors' misguided attempt to control what the rural should be, it would be important to adhere to the major tenets of critical pedagogy, those of empowering students and the instructor's role as facilitator rather than as classroom leader.

As envisioned by Haas and Nachtigal, this pedagogy also works counter to the current school reform movement, considering the constraints of NCLB that seek to measure all students against a statewide or nationwide set of outcomes. Additionally, these NCLB outcomes are to be measured with nationally parallel assessment tools. Rural students, who have just come through the K–12 system, may be especially sensitive to the tensions that arise between Haas and Nachtigal's proposed curriculum and their own recent experiences. I may be able to leverage their understanding of NCLB national standards, like the Common Core, against their knowledge of the rural with critical pedagogy in the classroom. I still have concerns about how to use critical pedagogy with students who may not consider themselves to be marginalized and align with the urban/suburban culture in a number of ways.

The work of Orr and of Haas and Nachtigal reflects differences in ideas for rural pedagogy and content that at times overlap, but all reflect a desire to use the rural K–12 school for some purpose that is likely to be more important to the authors than to the rural communities where these schools are located. There is a third way rural curriculum has been approached that more closely matches the will of and concerns of rural students, but which has not proven highly successful over time or replicable due to its reliance on local, situated knowledge and practices. Using the local geography and history as the center for curriculum was documented when Thomas Gjelten explored an expansion of the curriculum in Gary, Texas, that started in the early 1970s. Gjelten focused on the development of a *Foxfire*-style project, a publication conceived by high school teacher Lincoln King initially, but then developed, written, and distributed by students at the small rural school; the town's population was approximately two hundred when *Loblolly* began ("Gary, Texas" 227). Though the project was initially part of a tenth-grade geography class (230–32) it later became a journalism elective, which did not count toward graduation (233, 239).

Gjelten's article is a nuts-and-bolts examination of how this radical content and structure came to exist and gain status in the school as well as in the larger community. The content is student-generated and based in local geography, resources, history, and community. This would seem to answer a need for a rural curriculum, but *Loblolly* never served as anything more than an add-on. Gjelten reveals tensions between the academic curriculum, based in tradition and state examinations, and elective courses that are seen as important but not important enough to be included in graduation requirements. Despite the high status ascribed to the magazine, *Loblolly* is no longer being published. A last book of collected articles was published in 2005. Because the students' production of *Loblolly* did not mesh smoothly with state standards, it was doomed to be marginalized curricula, an interesting irony, and it only existed until the will of the teacher/advisor and students ran out. In this situation, rural pedagogy is equivalent to additional curriculum that exists more by the force of individual participants' will than by inclusion in the high school's overarching curricular goals.

Ultimately, my search for rural pedagogies has revealed few models from which I can draw to develop a more robust, critical pedagogy for use with my community college students. My search did reveal the complications that undergird teaching rural students, including control by outside-of-district agencies, the lack of discussion about rural students in higher education classes, and the economic pressures that determine the existence of small, rural schools. It is also clear that there is not a shared use or definition for rural pedagogy. The term is contested, taken over by pressures beyond what I would typically define as pedagogical, which I define as the work of teaching, the instructional methods employed in educating students. What little I found did not connect with critical pedagogy. As articulated in the introduction, critical pedagogy is important to me because rural students are often marginalized and subjected to cultural assumptions of the rural as a place and people of lack, lag, or a rosy past. In order to help students see themselves as legitimate members of the higher education community, to develop their skills in critical inquiry, to facilitate their use of critical thought to empower themselves, I need to be mindful of the needs of these students but go back to the roots of critical pedagogy in order to devise a critical rural pedagogy.

Requirements of Critical Rural Pedagogy for Rural Representation in First- and Second-Year College American Literature Courses

Key Characteristics of Good Rural Pedagogy

The fragmented nature of approaches to K–12 pedagogy for rural students does not provide adequate guidance for instructors when attempting to create a useful theoretical framework, let alone a useful pedagogical structure to use in a higher education class that includes student with rural backgrounds. I now offer a conversation on a possible pedagogy for students who have rural backgrounds in my community college, specifically, and in similar settings in higher education, more broadly. As I stated in the introduction, my book makes a case for theorizing rural literacy and developing critical pedagogy approaches for students who attend rural community colleges. As I outlined in Chapter 1, my own students have varied backgrounds, experiences, and socioeconomic statuses. I will now pick up these concerns, along with the importance of a critical pedagogy. What follows are my conceptions of and commitments to critical pedagogy. As stated in the introduction, critical pedagogy "works to help teacher educators and teachers reconstruct their work so it facilitates the empowerment of all students" (Kincheloe, *Knowledge* 9). For me, empowerment in this context means that rural students recognize the value of their contributions to class discussions and their academic work; that they believe they are not only welcome to share their ideas, but that their ideas need to be part of the conversations; and, lastly, that their rural knowledge can be useful not just for their own understanding of texts, but to add to the diversity of contexts and lenses through which a text can, and should, be examined.

The students in my classes have a variety of experiences, both in and out of the academic world, and are often disempowered by their social status, economic status, geographic location, age, ethnicity, or a number of other factors that have, at least in the eyes of some, relegated them to attending a community college in a poor, rural county of Washington state. Because I am working in a rural environment, it is also important to enact a critical rural pedagogy that 1) homes in to explore and use the language students bring from their rural lives into the classroom; 2) provides space for students to develop tactics and skills they can bring to bear when revealing biases that limit the rural or when speaking back against an author's representation of rural peoples and places; and 3) addresses students' positioning in multiple places concurrently in the power hierarchy, neither solely allied with the oppressor nor with the oppressed.

Use of Students' Language

In developing and theorizing critical rural pedagogy, I put forth the following key characteristics. First, a critical pedagogy would stress both the acceptance and the problematizing of students' use of language based in rural experience. Rural students bring particular vocabulary and language patterns that are not generally acknowledged in a higher education setting. For example, terms to denote specific ages, genders, and uses of livestock befuddle those who live in urban spaces. This complicated, rich understanding of animal husbandry is often mysterious to professors and classmates who have not lived in rural areas. Paulo Freire's thoughts on the teacher-student relationship, along with his criticisms of education as a bank rather than as a transformative experience (72), are helpful when approaching this gap. Creating classroom interaction where students are elevated from the oppressed to a position of some partnership in their learning, according to Freire, should enhance their learning experiences and would encourage them to share their rural knowledge and insights.

A move that counters a traditional construction of power and knowledge as top-down would create space for students to engage the texts using the language they already know, and allow them to apply their critiques and considerations to the texts without the overwhelming hand of authority from the professor with a "right" answer. This does not mean that any old thought a student expresses is perfection in its initial voicing, but it does mean that students have the power to voice their ideas and then refine their responses with continued discussion and exploration. As I picture an American literature class engaged in rural critical pedagogy, those students who have direct experience with the rural would hold a place of "expert" in aspects of a text's discussion that call for a critique of rural imagery, character development, and geography. Students' rural status and knowledge then become a significant asset in the richness of class discussions of texts with rural representations and peoples.

The difficulty may be not placing rural students with this knowledge in a position where they are asked to speak as a representative for all rural people, as happened in the vignette I shared earlier in this chapter. Instead, the opportunity to share this information has to be built over time. Trust and multiple chances for students to lead the direction of class discussion, to provide their expertise repeatedly in the classroom setting, has to occur in order for students to understand that their perspectives are important. Just as with critical pedagogy as a larger structure, critical rural pedagogy is not just a one-shot deal, a moment that only occurs when the text mentions a specifically rural location or person. Instead, it is a constant perspective, an openness, and an encouragement undergirding the entire class structure. When this is also a part of the classroom experience, students with rural expertise may share what they know first in pairs or in smaller groups where they are not on the spot before the entire class. Later, when trust is established and all students' individual contributions have been recognized and encouraged, students may choose to speak before the entire class but always as one additional perspective, not necessarily as the representative of a larger group. The construction of activities and discussions that provide a space for students to share what they know is also crucial for critical rural pedagogy to be successful.

David Bartholomae provides helpful insights on the difficulties of speaking and sharing in the academic world by providing for understanding the difficulties students face when entering higher education. The problem of "power and finesse," according to Bartholomae, lies in students' awareness of audience (595). Students from rural locations may lack awareness not only of the university setting, but also of the assumptions about rural and urban carried in the university environment. A highly urbanized space is constantly assumed to be "normal" on college campuses, making the rural students' background, by comparison, abnormal. Just as Bartholomae posits that prior texts are not able to help new writers (596), prior rural experiences may not inform the rural student in this new environment. Certainly, the use of Standard English in their previous academic lives is consistent, but there are aspects of their rural language that do not seem to be welcome in an urban space. The new urban, academic language does not include Carhartts, cattle squeezes, or distance as a factor in getting to stores, schools, and friends. So, in a critical rural pedagogy, I would seek curricular ways to include students' rural experiences, make links between their experience and the representations of the rural in literature, and develop critical thinking skills as they push within and against rural topoi as they encounter them in literature and their everyday life. I believe this would require instances of direct intervention early in the class to highlight the value of the variety of experiences students bring to the classroom. Later, it would become the instructor's job to facilitate the translation of language and themes from the lived rural into the academic language considered acceptable in university work. I will provide more specific examples of these pedagogical moves in Chapter 3.

Opportunities to Develop Tactics and Skills

In a critical rural pedagogy as I conceive it, giving students opportunities to develop tactics for building writing skills and critical thinking would be necessary. Activities, classroom discussion, written assignments, projects, and creative output would require instructors to design assignments that "provide the opportunity for engagement and growth" (Tinberg and Nadeau 116). Michel de Certeau's construction of strategies as opposed to tactics proves informative, illustrating possibilities for rural students to operate against the strategies of the larger educational structure or against economic systems based in a national view (34–39), where "strategies" are official rules and practices of government and cultural institutions (thus, are transparent, unchanging, rigid), and "tactics" are kairotic, situational, fly-by-the-seat-of-your-pants responses that may allow marginalized rural students to respond powerfully to their situation in college classrooms.

Ideally, a critical rural pedagogy should explore how and when rural students might use their prior knowledge to push back against simplistic understandings of the complicated, messy, and at times error-filled representations that appear in specific works of American literature. For example, as I mentioned briefly in Chapter 1, rural students did not bring their expertise into classroom discussion when we parsed the description of the Van Tassel farm in "The Legend of Sleepy Hollow," an impossibly productive and valuable homestead. The farm's amazing productivity, achieved with seemingly little effort on the part of the Van Tassel family, along with the often pristine environment presented in the tale, has much more to do with increasing the eligibility and desirability of the young Katrina Van Tassel than with the reality of a working farm. When Washington Irving's representation of a family farm is presented as accurate, rural students are in a unique position to complicate that interpretation of the text. Since rural students have not elected to share their expertise previously in my classroom, I hope to change that by providing tactics for intervening in that conversation that allow them to enter the critical discussion despite their at times perceived position of less power in the culture, and I hope to give them ways to "push off" from their first conversations into more complicated, complete, or rich discussions of the text as a whole, along with all their classmates, not just those who may have experiences in rural communities. Using de Certeau's construction of strategy and tactics, I can construct contexts, activities, and responses that may facilitate the full participation of rural students in the analysis of these American literature texts and, I hope, provide a way for rural students to see their varied, complicated experiences and intellectual gifts as both welcome and vital to success in the academic world.

Contextualizing Rural Students' Concurrent Positions of Power and Marginalization

And a critical pedagogy needs to contextualize students in their multiple positions, at times aligned with dominant culture and power, at other times, or perhaps concurrently, marginalized and othered. However, as pointed out in Chapter 1, rural students may not see themselves as outsiders, people whose lives are not automatically considered part of the dominant culture, despite the persistent and dominant representations of the rural that foreground what is missing, what is lagging behind, or what is connected with a fictionalized, mythic past forced upon rural students by government agencies, urban curriculum developers, and others, as demonstrated in Chapter 1. A critical rural pedagogy must take this paradox into account. I first looked at works by theorists and classroom practitioners who work with marginalized students in an attempt find guidance for how to construct classroom experiences that could navigate this difficult space.

The feminist pedagogical movement has significant insight into working with marginalized topics and peoples, especially when there are issues of power hierarchies and enshrined cultural attitudes. Melanie Kaye/Kantrowitz writes specifically about "teaching across difference" (281). She speaks directly to practices that allow students to "look for pockets of resistance, to understand how resistance is strengthened or undermined" (283). Her use of multiple lenses in the classroom to destabilize dominate theories, cultural constructs, and individual biases provides a model for an access point through which rural students may find an opportunity to voice more problematized interpretations of representations of the rural in texts and in their written analysis of such texts. Kaye/Kantrowitz opens her classes with overt conversations about hierarchy and power, as demonstrated in activities that require students to make the hierarchies of subgroups within the culture visible (285–86). This direct confrontation and isolation of the shadowy world of power that underlies the structure of American literature texts provides an entry point into the larger discussion later in the class. However, my concern with her approach is that my students may see themselves as connected to the "oppressor" group and resist the concerns of power and control because it may be considered an attack. While I find her direct approach appealing, I think that a more subtle approach, something that provides ways for students to discover for themselves the concerns of power that emerge from the literature, may be more effective. It may also take more time to build a sequence of activities that serve as small steps, allowing for tangents that are inevitable but also fruitful, because students should be driving toward discussions that have resonance for them. The representations of the rural are present in the literature, so students will most likely discover them, but tactics to arrive at this discovery may include patience on my part and recognition that this is not a straight line of reasoning. Instead, students will need to work through their revelations concerning the texts at their own pace, in their own way, if they are truly to be empowered.

My concerns were directly addressed by Mulholland, who, as discussed earlier, documents her experience working with preservice teachers in her article "For All Students in This Place." Mulholland provides a powerfully transparent record of her struggles in working with issues of native and non-native privilege, which I hoped to borrow to help illustrate the marginalization of rural students. Mulholland focuses on antiracist pedagogy but captures intentionality with a step-by-step system that offers a possible model. She combines a self-study activity, using student-created literacy biographies, with more direct instruction in "shared history and . . . post-colonial history" (197–99). This combination has created a space for explorations of privilege and the resulting consequences for those with and without privilege. A parallel series of assignments/conversations would be relatively easy to develop, using student-created literacy biographies as a contextualizing conversation around privilege in general, with follow-up activities to make explicit connections between the privilege students already identified in their autobiographies and the texts read in American literature.

I can also build upon Charlotte Hogg's chapter from *Rural Literacies*, "Beyond Agrarianism: Toward a Critical Pedagogy of Place," which activates Freire's theories and David Gruenewald's drive toward a "critical pedagogy of place . . . [focused on] decolonization and reinhabitation" (129–30). Although Hogg's critique of current agrarian ideas that can be traced back to Thomas Jefferson, with its embedded sexism, problematizes her initial work to create a rural pedagogy, the use of "specific social and economic contexts" she advocates can still be useful (128). Classroom discussions of literary works can include what she calls "the history of a rural area" (129). This history extends more than unilaterally through the narratives of people in a particular location. This history includes each particular area's economic and social connections with other geographical and political spaces. Connecting rural representations and peoples who appear in literary works with the more complicated world in which those texts were created and operated creates the scaffolding needed for richer conversations about texts.

While I will explore curricular possibilities further in the next chapter, for now let me say that instructors can develop activities and assignments that ask students to explore more deeply the histories of locations that appear in American literature. The students could be asked to create a finished version to present to the class in a number of modalities. Such an assignment could be expressed as a formal academic "researched" paper, as a multimodal visual presentation, or in another medium, such as song lyrics or poetry. The students' work then becomes the basis for comparison with the text, providing a structure with which to critique it. An advantage to this assignment is that students can find and trace the distinctions between the representation of the rural in the literature and the historical information that they have uncovered for themselves. Rather than a perceived attack on the dominant culture, if constructed carefully enough by the instructor, this activity has the advantage of using student-gathered information. That act both empowers the students by valuing their work and at the same time provides a way to see the power differentials and unpack the purposes authors may have had for creating particular representations of the rural.

In sum, let me distill the above into principles for a critical rural pedagogy as pedagogy that

- Explores and uses the language students bring from their rural lives into the classroom
- Provides space for students to develop tactics and skills they can bring to bear when revealing biases that limit the rural
- Addresses students' positioning across multiple places of power and marginalization with inquiry directed to understanding how this may be leveraged or may work against them in specific situations
- Accounts for top-down state standards, national benchmarks, and a general sense of "college readiness," but also adapts and situates pedagogical strategies, methods, and content to the students and their contexts
- Provides experiences that help students find their voices and become more empowered in the academic setting
- Recognizes that students will need to work through their own revelations concerning the texts in their own way, if they are truly to be empowered

From here, I move into a more pragmatic look at a community college classroom that embodies the above guiding principles for a rural critical pedagogy. Using a course from my campus, a first-year one-quarter survey of American literature, I present a series of activities and assignments that draw on the principles for critical rural pedagogy that I have developed. It is my hope that this practical exemplification will serve not only as a starting point for my own use of critical rural pedagogy in American literature, but also as a starting point for colleagues in similarly rural community colleges.

CHAPTER THREE

Classroom Activities and Examples

Vignette: The Giant Book

On the first day of my American literature class, I typically pull out the assigned anthology so my students can see the edition and cover of the book. It is common for me to hear an overwhelming vocal response. "Really, Dr. M? Are you seriously expecting us to bring this giant book to class every day?" accompanied with the requisite eye-rolling, shoulder-drooping, and open-mouthed gasps. These books are paperback, but they are not light and fluffy. They often have over a thousand pages on rice-paper-thin sheets. They could be used as door stops against hurricane-force winds. They cover works by American authors from before there was a United States right up to the present time, and often there is an attempt at breadth of the subject. A few students will have brought the text with them on the first day, but often they number fewer than half the class. Financial aid won't pay for books until a student has attended a first class. Other students have been stunned by the cost of the book, and they are waiting to see if they have to actually use the book in class, or whether they may be able to share with another person. Once the text is explored in the first class, I make it a point to use the book every single day. My students have a keen sense that if they have slapped down their hard-earned money, we had darned well better use the book.

Given the obvious difficulties in using a giant behemoth of a textbook, why would I assign it? Aren't there shorter texts, more limited in scope, or more focused on a theme, perhaps, to help students reach their course outcomes and objectives? Certainly, it would be reasonable to make that choice, but there are a number of restraints for instructors who teach Centralia College's American literature survey course (and, no doubt, at similar community colleges) which limits the textbooks that are most often assigned. Because the one-quarter introductory course needs to cover such a wide range of times, genres, authors, and topics, the large anthologies end up being more useful for the entire class and less expensive than assigning ten or fifteen individual texts. And there are multiple pressures that require first-year American literature courses to serve as wide-ranging surveys.

Why not use an open resource digital textbook? The price is certainly better for my students, but there are logistical concerns. My rural community college serves Lewis County, Washington, which covers 2,400 square miles, and only 80 percent of the homes in the county have access to broadband internet service ("Lewis County"). Additionally, the quality of that broadband service is spotty, a fact made especially evident when the college went to remote instruction starting in March of 2020 due to the COVID-19 pandemic. The college began to provide "hot spots" and laptops, but even with that help, some students were still going to local restaurant parking lots late in the evening to access free Wi-Fi with a stable signal. Those students who have not been able to connect remotely are simply not students any longer, so I have continued to choose a paper copy of the textbook. Those who have internet access may choose an e-version. This decision is not satisfying, but it does provide access to the greatest number of students. I intentionally use older editions so that students can purchase used copies, and our campus book loan program has helped defray these costs.

Access is only the first hurdle a text needs to clear. To begin with, the course needs to be "transferable" to a variety of other institutions of higher education in the state of Washington. When developing course outlines, individual instructors are required to check to be sure the course will be accepted when students transfer to the University of Washington, Washington State University, Western Washington University, Central Washington University, and

Eastern Washington University. A second set of colleges must also be consulted because students regularly transfer from Centralia College to The Evergreen State College, St. Martin's University, Pacific Lutheran University, and a host of other small, private colleges in the state. Often, if the University of Washington will accept a course for transfer, the other schools will follow its lead; however, this is not always the case. So, as much as possible, the content of the course must satisfy the wishes of each of these institutions. The result is that the course outline is a fairly general, and some would say traditional, survey of nineteenth- and twentieth-century American literature. To meet such a wide audience's needs, the anthologies are cost-effective, especially if using an older edition.

The need for the Centralia College American literature course to meet outside constraints is extended to the other community colleges in Washington because of common course numbering, overseen by the State Board for Community and Technical Colleges and legally required by the Washington state legislature since summer 2008 ("Common Course Numbering"). The course outlines are created on each campus, but there is no general consensus, other than course title, among community college campuses. While the content is not checked against the title officially, deans in the CCs monitor these courses as they are developed and the curriculum review committees on each local campus would not allow a course that has content dramatically mismatched with the title of the course. The transfer institutions either accept or do not accept the transfer credits for courses, and so again there is a tendency to go with the most traditional version of any course so that it will be acceptable to the greatest number of transfer colleges. The texts presented in an anthology have been accepted by the profession at large, so these anthologies become a common choice for first-year American literature surveys. Among other things, this means that pedagogies are formulated within these curricular constraints and preoccupations with course transfer.

Matching a general title to content may not seem overly limiting, but all courses at the community college level must pass an internal review by curriculum committees made up of stakeholders from across the campus that decide whether courses that are offered fit well with programmatic, budgetary, and scheduling needs of the rest of the college. That also means that despite an initial review by peers in a department, the ultimate "okay" for the course comes from a committee made up of people who are not content-area specialists. The collegiality and professionalism of these committees, while often of the highest level, depends heavily on the administrator in charge to set limits for questions concerning course outlines and the tone of these conversations. When confronted with a hostile committee, course outlines may migrate to the "safest" version of the course, which means the most traditional, since other faculty are remembering courses they took as undergraduates five to forty years before. American literature is, unfortunately, a course that other faculty members believe themselves to be somewhat knowledgeable about, providing for more meddling in course content than in, say, a statistics course or a nursing course.

On my campus, there is one remaining area of constraint. Because we are a relatively small campus, in 2020 enrolling 1,900 full-time students, of whom 900 are enrolled in college transfer courses and programs, there are limited offerings for American literature ("About Centralia College"). There is only one American literature course, one non Western world literature course, one women's literature course, and one British literature course offered at the first- and second-year level. These courses are surveys precisely so that the few students who will be majoring in literary studies at their transfer institutions have a wide enough background to facilitate some general understanding of the overall patterns of literature before they move on to upper-division courses. For all students transferring on after completing their associate of arts degree, survey literature courses may fulfill part of their general requirements.

So, given all of this, the large anthology, for good or ill, is the best tool for meeting the needs of the course outline and the financial constraints for students. While these texts serve these purposes well, there is a curricular concern. Typically, students use the book as their only real reference. While this is not what I would encourage if these students were English majors, most are not. I bring in additional materials to the classroom, but the time constraints of the large survey course and students' often limited interest in the content generally make adding reading assignments outside of the textbook a less successful approach. The students have limited financial resources and time. As is typical for community college students, they are often working at least part-time and may be caring for siblings or other family members. While the ideal would be to include multiple and frequent additional materials, it is important to make the best use of the materials that are immediately available, in this case, the major textbook for the class.

The ancillary materials in the anthologies typically include a preface, introductions to sections of the book, introductions to specific authors, and occasional web resources or end-of-section questions. While I can encourage and support students who read the ancillary materials, David Bartholomae's comments are an important reminder of the impact of reading only one perspective on any work of literature. Once students begin to write about that text, "[t]he act of writing, here, has a personal cognitive history . . . that is made possible by prior texts," and reading research, Bartholomae continues, makes it "possible to say that these prior texts, or a reader's experience with these prior texts, have bearing on how the text is read" (596). If students have read the ancillary materials prior to reading/discussion/class activities/writing activities, then what appears in these ancillary materials and introductions form part of the students' reactions. If students have had limited exposure to these types of texts or have only seen one example, from an anthology, for example, their thinking about these texts will be shaped by the language they have seen used and are attempting to replicate to some degree in their own responses to the literary works.

Because these ancillary materials will be the place where students look first for information on the assigned works, it is important to make a brief, closer examination of the ancillary materials in three major American literature anthologies that I might use in this first-year survey course. The three dominant topoi of lack, lag, and rosy past (Donehower et al., *Rural Literacies* 1) appear in the editors' written texts that frame and contextualize these anthologies. Because the three topoi appear often in the ancillary materials, they serve as a readily available frame that can be used in critical rural pedagogy designed to help students challenge thin or simplistic rural representations. Rather than simply accepting the information and contexts for the literary texts as presented in the ancillary materials, students should be able to talk back to, contest, and question these presentations of text. I should provide activities that assist students to recognize and push back against these representations of the rural. I have included one example activity for each of the three major anthologies.

Analyzing Ancillary Materials in Anthologies

I have chosen to examine the ancillary materials found in American literature anthologies, focusing on American literary works that have met two criteria. First, they must be works that can be taught according to the Centralia College American literature course outline. My current course outline does reflect the most conservative, or traditional, approach to the content of an introductory American literature course. Second, specific works are included because they have characters, imagery, narrative, or settings that highlight rural areas or small towns. The following examples work well for rural students who have the experiences that allow them to recognize when the texts' representations of the rural do and do not match their knowledge of rural peoples and places. Three works that meet these criteria are authored by Henry David Thoreau, Robert Frost, and Flannery O'Connor. I will also briefly address the degree to which similar constructions of the rural are dominant in the ancillary materials for the three chosen authors/works across three typical textbooks on my campus, the shorter *Norton Anthology of American Literature*, edited by Nina Baym (2008); the Pearson *Concise Anthology of American Literature*, edited by George McMichael and James S. Leonard (2006); and the *Heath Anthology of American Literature*, edited by Paul Lauter (2009).

When presenting these authors' works, the three anthologies follow similar though not identical patterns. All three include excerpts from Thoreau's *Walden*: "II: Where I Lived and What I Lived For," "XVII: Spring," and "XVIII: Conclusion." Each anthology includes fourteen to sixteen individual poems by Robert Frost. Poems that appear in all three are: "Mending Wall," "The Road Not Taken," "Stopping by Woods on a Snowy Evening," and "Design." Each of the anthologies included only one O'Connor short story. Two included "Good Country People," while the *Heath Anthology* included "A Good Man Is Hard to Find." Later in this chapter, I will be sharing activities that explore these texts, as well as Alice Walker's "Everyday Use," which appears in the *Norton Anthology*.

It is important to remember who uses the ancillary materials that accompany these authors' works and how that might alter the students' understandings. Students are expected to refer to these sections to add context and depth to their understanding of authors' texts. Realistically, in a lower-division American literature course, most students are not literature majors. Those with a declared major or a special interest in the subject will read these materials, but the rest of the class may not. A few students will read the ancillary materials and not the assigned text. Although editors of these texts hope students will read these materials, there also is a second audience. Instructors, teaching assistants, and professors will also refer to these materials. Including this information can then enhance sales of the books because they offer support for those teaching the classes who may have limited pedagogical training or experience with such a wide range of texts.

This secondary audience is visible in the editor's inclusion of a timeline showing what has come before and what will come later, specific literary techniques or stylistic contributions to be found in the selected texts by each author, and often additional references. Few general studies students care that there are other, more specific books to read about each author and their works. However, for the new teaching assistant who is using an anthology for the first time, the adjunct instructor who was just handed the anthology and course outline days before the start of the course (not unusual in community colleges), or the professor who is teaching outside the narrow band of their expertise, these introductory and ancillary materials are a godsend. Ancillary materials are read carefully, notes are taken, and, at times, these materials drive pedagogy.

As a genre, ancillary materials in anthologies have specific features and limitations. The introductory materials must serve multiple audiences. The long-time instructor approaches the textbook as one who "knows" and just needs a brief refresher or as a person who clearly knows much more than can be written into the introduction and may be critical of this information as a reader. The editor also needs to consider these readers, too. What will other professors think of the approach used in the ancillary materials? Does it play to a particular strand of thinking in the field—political, theoretical, student-centered, critical in its stance to a particular subfield of study? Meanwhile, for the publisher, introductions must be features that "sell" the book. Introductions to each work need to take up a minimal number of pages, due to publishing costs, yet need to be the feature that, in part, draws instructors' attention. Ancillary materials need to help with sales yet must not make the textbook too expensive. This is a tricky line to walk and necessitates a generalization of concepts and often a macroview of materials. Finally, ancillary materials need to be clearly organized to help students interpret and place the text that follows within a particular time frame, social context, and theoretical framework.

As a result, the ancillary materials follow an editor's prescribed pattern, which is replicated throughout the anthology. The editor builds the illusion of a single text rather than a collection of random texts bound together. For the editor, the question becomes how much parallel structure is enough. Whatever the choices, the remaining piece should match the pattern, limiting the editor's options in the ancillary materials. The ancillary materials need to be written at a first-year college reading level, with enough interesting construction to hold students' attention. These students may not know much about the texts or the authors, so the information must be clear and relatively comprehensive. It helps if it can pique interest, telling enough to make a student curious to do more reading on their own. References to others' works is a standard inclusion, but copious in-text citations or footnotes make the introductory texts much less readable, so editors most often provide a brief list of reference materials at the end of each introduction.

In terms of representations of the rural, literature anthologies also reflect the general cultural use of lack, lag, and rosy past when introducing texts in their ancillary materials. Although I could do a full analysis of the anthologies to support this assertion, given the focus of this book on pedagogy, it is more useful here to provide a typical example and then to focus on how to use them in the context of a critical rural pedagogy approach. In the *Concise Anthology of American Literature*, the introductory section "The Age of Romanticism" (McMichael and Leonard 399–403) frames the rural as a place without cultural value on its own merits. Instead, the intro materials suggest that urban authors were necessary to bring the rural out of its low, culturally unimportant, or lacking, position. As the editors explain, "American character types speaking local dialects appeared in poetry and fiction with increasing frequency. Literature began to celebrate American farmers, the poor, the unlettered, children, and noble savages (red and white) untainted by society" (403). It is interesting to note how the farmer has become an outsider, marginalized with the rest of the people in this list. The rural person is not part of the mainstream although most people still lived in rural environments until 1910, according to the US census, well after the Age of Romanticism is considered over by academics. In 1910, 54.4 percent of the population was classified as living in rural environments, and by 1920 that number had dropped to 48.8 percent ("Population"). By comparison, in 1860, 80.2 percent were classified as rural, while in 1990, the percentage of the US population classified as rural had dropped to 24.8 percent ("Population"). The editor seems to be reflecting an impression dominant in the modern world, namely that rural spaces are inhabited by people who were left behind, who are not up-to-date, or who are on the edges of society rather than examining these ideas through the historical context of a predominantly rural population.

The concepts of lack, lag, and rosy past create a bias that will not help instructors who are unfamiliar with the rural, especially if they are, as discussed in Chapter 2, "transient exotic" professors (Zencey 16), who are not from rural settings and, therefore, might be less attentive to this minimization of the rural. In fact, the ancillary materials potentially reinforce the marginalization of rural students' experiences in the world of higher education. Because ancillary materials are a shortened written form, varying in length from a short paragraph to a page or two, it is not surprising that the language reveals an embedded bias that depicts the rural simplistically and that draws on commonplace representations of the rural. This constructed representation is reinforced, and students are expected to accept lack, lag, and rosy past, as true. Kenneth Burke's terministic screen is helpful for understanding that these materials are written by people who are not attuned to the complexities of rural life, and therefore they rely on the more simplistic bias of the larger culture, which prioritizes the urban. The term "rural" directs the attention of these writers to the culturally dominant definition, for as Burke states, "Even if any given terminology is a reflection of reality, by its very nature as a terminology it must be a selection of reality; and to this extent it must function also as a deflection of reality" (45). Although the understanding of the term *rural* expressed in the ancillary materials is not false, it reflects only one understanding of the reality of the rural, or, as Burke describes, the same object may be observed through a different "color filter, with corresponding differences in the nature of the event as perceived, recorded, and interpreted" (46).

Examples of this limited representation of the rural are abundant in each of the anthologies' ancillary materials for Thoreau, Frost, and O'Connor. Rural students' more complicated understanding of who lives in rural spaces, how people interact with others in rural areas, and what occurs in those spaces does not appear in American literature texts that foreground rural locations and peoples. My greatest concern is the likelihood that rural students will "read" themselves as outside of the academic landscape. They will not see themselves in these works. Additionally, because they are first- and second-year students (who may be aged from sixteen to sixty), they may or may not have the experience or confidence in academic settings to contest these depictions or see the classroom as an opportunity for making productive connections between course content and their everyday lives.

In order to complicate the anthologies' limited depictions of the rural in the context of a critical rural pedagogy, I offer in this chapter classroom activities, writing assignments, and interactive experiences with the authors' works that move beyond the ancillary materials while taking advantage of the topoi of lack, lag, and rosy past, culturally resonant ideas that students can contest. They can explore how these terms are controlled, deployed, and perhaps resisted in texts, and how their use by authors reflects deliberate minimizing strategies or culturally embedded attitudes. The speed and breadth of content coverage in a survey course are important when considering how students will be asked to work. Generally, individual texts are read by students before the one class in which the work is discussed. Then, students move on to the next text, read before the next class session, which will also be accorded one class session before moving on. This is a breakneck pace. Every class session and assignment needs to make the best possible use of time and energy. Despite the fact that there are multiple ways to approach each text, and because so many students are not English majors, interactive class activities become especially important. With that in mind, the following activities and assignments serve as examples for what may be achieved within the confines of time and student expertise in the subject area. My goal is to provide a sampling of what is possible and how an American literature survey course might make use of critical rural pedagogy. Through the next two sections, I will provide examples for taking advantage of a critical reading of the anthology ancillary materials, and then I will share activities for use with the literary texts for the remainder of the chapter.

Opening Activities to Prepare for Critical Rural Pedagogy

The opening day of class presents an interesting opportunity, not only to set the tone for the work to come but to engage students in challenging assumptions they may have about the range of experiences their classmates bring to future discussions and analysis of American literature. It is important when teaching with a critical rural pedagogy that students see their rural experiences as central. Each student's experiences are to be valued, included, and encouraged when supporting, contesting, or speaking back to the representations of the rural later in the class. In order to set this tone, I use the "Who Has . . . " game to reveal the variety of student experiences and expertise without placing any one student in a position of being the sole representative of a particular group or making shy students uncomfortable. Even at this early point, the idea of rural students as a static or homogenous group can begin to be chipped away. At the start of the activity, each student gets a pile of paper. I often use 3x5 cards, cut in half. As each question is asked, those students who have the experiences repeat or describe the experiences on a slip of paper. In a digital class space, I will ask students to submit their answers to me privately via assignment submission so they are all in one place. After students have responded, I share back to the class how many of the items on the list are experiences of their classmates. I do not reveal names or numbers of responses for each. This is important for ensuring that students know they control their individual information in this class. Building class community includes ensuring a sense of security.

I also participate in this activity so that I can model an initial response and so that my experiences will also be added to the general class knowledge. For example, I may begin with "Who has traveled outside the United States?" and model a possible answer, emphasizing that students may add details if they wish. Once all the questions have been asked and answered, I collect the slips, and as a group we see what experiences we will be able to draw from in our class. Additionally, this activity makes visible individual student experiences while providing support for all experiences and their value as perspectives that will help make discussion of the texts more complicated and interesting. This opening activity also works well because it does not diminish the experiences of individual students. Instead, the importance of each person's contributions to class becomes the baseline from which class discussion will operate. A variety of questions might include "Who has______?":

- Traveled outside the United States
- Lived on a farm
- Taken a subway
- Worked full-time
- Attended a small high school
- Attended a large high school
- Attended private school
- Attended home schooling
- Lived in a ranch-style house
- Eaten food you have grown/raised
- Had children
- Been the primary person responsible for siblings
- Spoken more than one language
- Figured out how to get around with a city bus or rail schedule
- Traveled on a train
- Ridden a horse
- Owned or cared for livestock
- Owned a car
- Shared ownership of a car
- Worked for family, without pay

This in-class activity activates the guidelines for rural critical pedagogy, creating a space in which rural vocabulary and experiences are valued equally within the classroom setting, making evident the previously unseen details of their classmates' experiences, creating a more complicated understanding of the academic setting, and developing a context for the position of rural students in the dominant societal representations. When the complexity and variety of experiences are made visible, students have concrete evidence that the rural, as a place that is lacking, lagging behind, and/or a reflection of a rosy past, can be directly called into question. The next step is to ask students to create a definition of a rural person, based on the information their classmates have provided in this activity. I often ask students to work in small groups so that at the end of the activity there are multiple definitions. The conversation with classmates allows for multiple conversations while creating a limited number of definitions for us to examine in more detail as a class if there is time.

As with most pedagogical moves, this one activity does not completely develop all aspects of the guidelines for critical rural pedagogy. This activity is not intended to serve as a separate or finalizing conversation. Instead, the "Who has______?" game is one small part of a longer-term series of intellectual opportunities for students to enrich their sense of the world and how they are defined or seen. Additionally, this activity is one of numerous chances for students to practice making direct comparisons between what is represented about the rural and their own experiences. Professors can develop intellectual structures that will help students to express and explore these complications. For example, just a few of these structures might include short definitions or comparison-contrast charts that then lead to prose expressions of those same ideas, adding details to a statement and citing from another text to support a statement. With this opening activity, students can begin to orient their own ideas and experiences of the rural within the ideas that circulate in the dominant culture. This activity also opens a space for recognizing that individuals may occupy multiple positions of power, as depicted in their rural definitions and highlighted through instructor-led discussion. Critical pedagogy encourages students to call into question the hegemonic structures in place around them over time, and the guidelines I have proposed for critical rural pedagogy do the same, with an enhanced focus on a particular subset of experiences pertaining to the rural without minimizing other experiences students bring to the classroom setting.

Activities to Problematize Anthology Introductions to Thoreau, Frost, and O'Connor

I also include more specific activities that encourage students to speak back to, to question, and to complicate the information they are given in the introductions. Because, as noted earlier, the textbook's ancillary materials might be the only context students have for each American literature text the class covers, critical rural pedagogy can be useful in helping students see those texts as only one, limited way to envision the rural. I have included one example of a classroom activity to accompany an introduction from each of the most common anthologies mentioned earlier: *The Norton Anthology of American Literature* (Baym), the *Concise Anthology of American Literature* (McMichael and Leonard), and the *Heath Anthology of American Literature* (Lauter). I do use older editions of anthologies in order to save costs for students.

The Norton Anthology of American Literature (2008) has a five-page introduction to the works of Henry David Thoreau. Because the text is particularly dense, it is helpful to isolate a specific section of the introduction for closer examination by students. One in-class exercise gives students tools for exploring the information and language used by the introduction's author. I have pulled one small section of the introduction, which students often read too quickly or not at all. The language is inserted in the chart below, which is then distributed to students in class. Ideally, students would work through this activity in groups of two or three so that a variety of responses can be gleaned and so that all students participate. In a digital synchronous class, students can work in breakout rooms with their groups. In an asynchronous digital class, students can work on a shared cloud document, such as a Google Doc. The principles of critical rural pedagogy enacted in this activity include situating the strategies to the students and their context, helping students express their ideas, and exploring the language students bring with them from their rural lives to the classroom. Students need not complete every "box," but instead I encourage them to focus on those they feel most comfortable with or are ready to respond to during the short class period or limited asynchronous timeline. The idea here is to initiate thinking about the introduction more precisely and to speak back to the text.

From the introduction (Baym, 825–26)	Central Idea	How would you rephrase this for a friend?	Does this language suggest lack, lag, or rosy past (Donehower et al., *Rural Literacies* 1)? How?	How have you seen this depiction of the rural appear in public discourse or popular culture?	How does this depiction match or not with your own experiences with and perceptions of the rural?
To his great embarrassment, during a camping trip in April of that year, he accidentally set fire to the Concord woods near Walden Pond, burning approximately three hundred acres and causing over $2,000 in damage.					
Shortly after this event, Thoreau decided to begin what he termed his "experiment" at Walden, building a cabin on land that Emerson owned near the pond					

and taking up residence there on July 4, 1845—a symbolic moment of personal liberation aligned with the celebration of national freedom.					
One of Thoreau's major goals in moving to the pond was to write a book about his 1839 boating journey with his brother (which he completed before he left after two years, two months, and two days).					
Only a couple of miles from town, his cabin became the destination of many local visitors, and he often went back to Concord for meals and conversation.					
These events are recorded in *Walden* but the effect of its descriptions of Thoreau alone at the pond—and the book's frequently confrontational tone—were such that many readers are surprised to learn that Thoreau could, after all, be sociable.					

By the middle of the twentieth century, Thoreau's literary reputation equaled or surpassed Emerson's, with *Walden* regarded as one of the masterpieces of American literature.					
It is a work that has powerfully affected environmentalists like John Muir and Aldo Leopold, who greatly admired Thoreau for his concerns about the natural habitat.					

By responding to these questions, students will be improving their skills in close reading, an important goal of the course, and the last four columns provide ways for students' own language to be highlighted and sought after in the discussion that follows the group work. The topoi of lack, lag, or rosy past are also enacted. By following the pair work with a larger discussion or by asking two groups to share their work with each other, the ways students conceptualize terms that may be regarded differently in a variety of contexts may be brought out. A more extended essay assignment could follow the in-class use of the questions and form presented above. Students could next be asked to explore the ways that terms such as those used in the introduction have complicated interpretations, including "environmentalists," "natural habitat," "pond," "cabin," and "camping." For example, the students' conception of a cabin is open to wide variation in a rural setting, and even more so when students' ideas about cabins are compared with photographs of Thoreau's replicated cabin, which are readily available through the internet.

Another distinction in representations to be explored is Thoreau's "natural habitat," which closer examination reveals is actually a domesticated rural landscape that had been significantly altered by the presence of farmers, country roads, and people's need to make a living. There are ponds that have been created or eliminated, fences that have been erected, and little outbuildings like his cabin that have been built. Students may have an impression of a "natural habitat" that is much less altered by people. An assignment that directs students to make comparisons with Thoreau's use of several of these terms with the use of these terms in the present time, along with examples, gives students an opportunity to improve their writing abilities, their analysis of text, and how these texts may relate to parallel ideas in a modern context. These comparisons may be written in a formal paper or expressed in a multimodal form.

A second anthology, the *Concise Anthology of American Literature* (2006), has much shorter introductions to authors' works. The introduction for Robert Frost is not quite a full page (McMichael and Leonard 1537). One way to question the representation in this introduction is to ask students to mark each instance where the introduction suggests something about Frost that strikes them as "negative" and something that strikes them as "positive." For example, the editors state, "Frost eked out a minimal living by teaching and farming while continuing to write his poems" (1537). Frost was unable to make a living both farming and teaching? The editors point out that Frost had to leave, in fact to go all the way to London, to be culturally recognized. The implied solution is to abandon the rural location and go to where there is culture. This is especially problematic for rural students because they will recognize the complicated aspects of rural life that Frost foregrounds and explores in his poems. The editors posit that "[t]o his rural New England neighbors, Robert Frost was an unlikely farmer who wrote poetry into the late hours and milked his cows at midnight. To much of the American public, he was a white-thatched, rustic sage, a poet of rural simplicity and public virtue" (1537). While this section makes clear a positive image of Frost connected to virtue, the combination of this image with "rural simplicity" complicates the connotation and gives students an opportunity to explore the ways that language of this introduction flattens the rural world Frost himself is attempting to capture.

Frost's poems illustrate, in part, the complexity of a life that appears quiet and still from the outside but is built on turmoil, violence, variation, and dynamism. The editors also conflate the language of his poems with supposedly rural speech patterns: "He employed the plain speech of rural New Englanders and preferred the short, traditional forms of lyric and narrative" (1537). This sense of Frost as superficial and simplistic is immediately contrasted with a statement that suggests surprise that Frost's poems have deeper meaning: "[H]is concern with nature reflected deep moral uncertainties, and his poetry, for all its apparent simplicity, often probes mysteries of darkness and irrationality in the bleak and chaotic landscapes of an indifferent universe where men and women stand alone, forsaken and perplexed" (1537). When students "flag" the language that strikes them as negative or positive, they open up a possible conversation around why these ideas carry emotional impressions, whether the negative/positive impression varies depending on the audience, and how they might alter the language to reflect a less biased representation of Frost's writing life. This in-class exercise will then provide leverage for a more in-depth discussion or a short reflective writing at the end of the class session. The editor's idealization of the rural past cannot be sustained when the poems' themes and structures are carefully examined. Unfortunately, the continuous use of the representations of a rural past that was idyllic remains in use, even by careful academics. By pushing back against these embedded representations in the introduction, students are better able to come to Frost's poems with a more complicated understanding of the rural than that it provides, and that lens does not reduce their expectations for Frost's range of emotions and complicated depictions in poetic form.

The third commonly used anthology I will consider is the *Heath Anthology of American Literature* (2009). Flannery O'Connor's work appears in *Volume E: Contemporary Period, 1945 to the Present*, and the introduction is a little more than a page long (Lauter 2567–68). The introduction does not focus on the rural. There is a slight, almost offhanded, rural reference to the end of O'Connor's life: "But mostly she lived quietly on the farm [after 1950]—until surgery in February 1964 reactivated the lupus; she died in August at the age of 39" (2567). There is no conversation or exploration of her deeper connection with the rural place where she lived and died. The only other moment that touches on the rural points out what is missing: "Yet her characters are not so much fallen aristocrats as poor or middle-class whites, who often don't realize that their lives are lacking" (2567). The blunt statement about what is missing and how people are too backward and simple even to realize what is not in their lives can be read as an insult by rural students. I was stunned to discover that the introductory materials on O'Connor's work did not see the rural locations of her stories as important enough for commentary. The students in my American literature classes have always identified with O'Connor, sometime quite forcefully, as a rural author. Despite the distance between Washington State and the southern United States, my rural students have spoken about her works with a sense of connection, a recognition that the difficult situations she creates not only could happen in rural spaces but in rural areas where they live. Her descriptions of rural spaces, her use of local speech patterns, and her choice to explore complicated ideas through rural characters resonate with students.

Enacting a direct approach to complicating the missing rural in this introduction, I can ask students to complete a short, in-class activity. I have included the instructions below.

"Yet her characters are not so much fallen aristocrats as poor or middle-class whites, who often don't realize that their lives are lacking" (Lauter 2567) is a statement in the introduction to Flannery O'Connor in our textbook. If you were to write a short story set in a rural location, what other sorts of characters could you include? Make a list of people who could populate your story. Be prepared to share your list with the class in discussion. Why have you included these characters/types of people?

Such lists are the first of several steps that give students a way to capture the more complex variety of people they are familiar with in rural areas. By asking them to write them down in a list form, the complexity may be captured, though not completely. The next step is to combine the lists in a format where all students can comment, interact, and add to the discussion. A whiteboard or shared electronic space works well. If there is time, a follow-up to this activity asks students to more fully develop at least one of the characters that have been briefly identified in the class list. This activity again highlights the importance of students' language and knowledge of the rural world, providing a space in an academic classroom where their knowledge adds to the value of the intellectual discussion. This is an important principle in critical rural pedagogy. When there is time, a follow-up written assignment puts students into groups of two or three and asks them to write a short fictional piece in which their characters interact.

In an assignment that further pushes against the biased view of the rural as a place where the people are simplified or flattened in textual representations, students are asked to find a person they find interesting from the local community and then share this person with the class through digital storytelling. The impetus to find someone who is "interesting" should focus students on sharing their knowledge of real people from the community who have caught the students' attention. The process of choosing a person brings each group into an important internal conversation about what is interesting. Is this person doing something surprising? Is this person doing something familiar in an especially intriguing way? The need to discover and then share more than a surface representation achieves several of the goals for a critical rural pedagogy, including giving students an opportunity to create and share their own rural representations and helping them to develop tactics and skills that reveal the limiting biases regarding the rural and speak back against those biases. While the required pace of the class may prohibit the use of this last portion of the assignment, it may be possible to offer this as an enrichment assignment for those who can take the time.

Activities That Enact Critical Rural Pedagogy: Activities for Texts in an American Literature Classroom

College Classroom as Context

My Centralia College students' diversity of experiences is often reflected in the variety of their clothing. There are younger, running-start/dual-enrolled students who wear high school letter jackets, logoed high school t-shirts, and hoodies, and older students may have just come from or are headed off to work, wearing suits or parts of a uniform, with dress shoes. Others wear actual pajama bottoms and slippers along with an oversized sweatshirt. There are those who dress to attract the attention of their classmates and those who dress not to be noticed. There are designer handbags and Walmart sale bags. Another clothing pattern in my classes is Carhartt jackets and field boots, frequently with remnants of those fields still adhering to that footwear. The students in Carhartts also often have "gimme" hats from the feed store, and their jeans have tears and holes from encounters with barbed-wire fences or from irritated farm animals or from just having been worn for too long. There are worn leather work gloves in their pockets. The question for me, as their instructor, then becomes how to engage all my students and to find pedagogically sound activities that, when appropriate, draw on the use of lack, lag, and rosy past as dominant topoi for deeply critical readings of texts. I need to use contexts, activities, and assignments that will allow rural students to draw on their expertise.

After having explored the ancillary materials and clearly noted that those materials replicate the dominant ideas of the rural as places of lack, lag, and/or a rosy past, it is clear that students in my rural community college who enroll in the American literature survey course could benefit from an interventionist deployment of critical rural pedagogy. I use the theoretical framework I offered in Chapter 2, critical rural pedagogy, which encourages students from rural areas to develop their intellectual voices in the college classroom, empowers them to bring their experiences into their discussions and coursework, and helps them to begin to sort through the complicated power dynamics of being part of a dominant cultural group while recognizing the ways that, as rural students, they may also occupy a position that has been marginalized over time. I now provide examples for classroom activities that reflect a pedagogy that encourages rural and small-town students in the class to share their expertise. Ideally, students will be able to deploy their experiences and their developing knowledge of the constructed nature of these texts (made by a person for a particular reason, not a transcendent rendering of "truth") to problematize and enrich their interactions with American literature texts that foreground the rural in their locations and characters. Having these additional perspectives voiced should add to, not overwhelm or diminish, other voices in academic discussions, whether at the community college level or at transfer universities. Additionally, I hope rural students might recognize the value of their experiences in an academic world that at times may be oblivious of or even hostile to rural experiences.

Providing a context that frames the college class and identifies the importance of representation, power structures, and the way students may see themselves in relation to these ideas is an important step toward creating an ongoing conversation for the length of the class. One activity, modeled on the work of Melanie Kaye/Kantrowitz, who writes about teaching across differences (285–86), helps students to contextualize hegemonic structures that appear in the works, and prompts more critical interplay between all the texts read over the course. First, using the syllabus, students identify all the texts to be read in the anthology. Generally, the reading list in the American literature survey includes twenty to thirty authors, with one or two readings from most authors. These authors and their work represent multiple geographic locations, as well as social and economic classes. In small groups, starting with only the clues of titles and general overview in the ancillary materials, students begin to compile a chart that points out various identity markers (language, dress, social status, race, geography) from the characters and settings. Since this is an ongoing assignment, which will be revisited periodically, not all the texts assigned need to be examined in one sitting. Instead, this chart can be revised. However, it is important that each session of this activity end with placing characters and or places on a visual hierarchy. Converting this information from text into images, even if they are minimalist stick people above and below each other on a whiteboard, gives some students another entry point into their understanding of the power structures that are embedded in American literature. The visual aspect of this assignment can also work well as a digital map, created by the class in a shared electronic space, like a Google or other cloud document.

The combination of the chart or map to illustrate a visual hierarchy may serve well as a jumping-off point for written assignments that address questions such as: What do these stories suggest about who has power, who keeps power, who gains power, and whether that system should change? For those texts that include rural characters and locations, this assignment provides a scaffold for all students to notice how the rural is constructed and gives students with rural experiences an invitation to bring that knowledge to bear as they discuss the implications of this visual hierarchy on the rural images texts create.

Example Class Activities and Assignments

In the remainder of this chapter, I will provide examples of activities that may be used when teaching Henry David Thoreau's "Where I Lived and What I Lived For" from *Walden,* Robert Frost's "Mending Wall," Flannery O'Connor's "Good Country People," and Alice Walker's "Everyday Use." While it is possible to include many more activities and works, I have chosen to highlight the following as examples of what might be accomplished when using a critical rural pedagogy. I have chosen these specific texts because they explicitly foreground rural imagery, people, or places, providing a clear path for the connection with and/or contestation against these representations by my rural community college students. It is my intention to provide five or six options that could be useful with each of these selected texts. It is my hope that instructors would be able to adapt these ideas to their teaching contexts.

I can't do all of these activities and assignments in a ten-week quarter, but I can pull from these options as the culture of a specific class emerges. This allows me to tailor the activities to the students' interests, experiences, and strengths.

Henry David Thoreau's "Where I Lived and What I Lived For" from Walden

When approaching Thoreau, students often have a surface understanding of his work, having read portions of his work in either high school government or American literature classes, but I would like them to interrogate the text with a more critical eye. Below I describe an activity, which may start in the classroom and then move into students' own reflective writing or formal essay, that focuses on Thoreau's attitude toward property ownership. Students begin in small groups, ideally two to four people per group, and examine Chapter 2 of *Walden*, "Where I Lived and What I Lived For." They are to pay special attention to the language and attitudes Thoreau displays about farmers, property ownership, and farming versus gardening. Guiding questions for their discussion, which may be projected on a screen for the class, printed on a handout, or shared on a digital slide in an LMS include:

What is the hierarchy Thoreau presents?

Who is elevated in this hierarchy?

What does Thoreau identify as the purpose for land ownership? How does this sense of ownership match or not with your own or other attitudes toward land ownership that you have encountered?

What does this passage illustrate about Thoreau's personal experiences with rural spaces?

How might Thoreau's discussion change if he were dependent on land for his economic survival or if he had a family to support?

Critical rural pedagogy helps to position this assignment in a way that encourages students who come from farming or landowning families to articulate their perspective on what ownership means against Thoreau's conception. Students who do not have experiences that complicate Thoreau's depictions and attitudes are also provided a context for looking at Thoreau's work from a "use of land" perspective. Students can bring their language and knowledge to the forefront of this discussion, allowing for a more robust analysis of the concept of property, not just as a label, but also to explore the cultural connections of property to power and prestige within a community. This pushback against the text helps students recognize the limits of Thoreau's ideology, and the exercise also asks all students to consider what is both revealed and obscured by Thoreau's perspective.

A second approach that may be used builds on Thoreau's use of the term "sublime," which suggests an elevated, perhaps spiritual understanding of the transcendent power and beauty of natural space. Most often, he uses the term without definition. A classroom activity that requires students to find all the uses of the term in the selection and then attempt to explain what he might mean when using the word in each example provides for a concrete structure in which students get a chance to practice their close reading skills and to develop their understanding of the rural world as Thoreau constructs it. The variations of his use of the term and how that use conflates a natural setting with a rural, cultivated setting reveal the ways that rural spaces are created for particular purposes in literature.

A follow-up written assignment asks students to compare Thoreau's use of the word "sublime" with another text of their choice that uses the word, though perhaps with a different meaning. A number of texts would work, ranging from blogs and poetry discovered in a digital search to articles that extol the beauty and experience of skiing and hiking. The term has multiple meanings, which students may not have considered closely before. The essay assignment on Thoreau's work makes the representation of land that is free of or inhabited by limited numbers of people as having an exalted status is a point of contention in modern rural spaces. Rural communities often want to use land to produce a living, while those from out of the area may wish to preserve the same land, at times at the expense of those who are living in the area under dispute.

These negotiations and at times direct conflicts around land use also have the feature of language that creates a particular context. The topoi of rosy past can rise to the surface and structure the ongoing disputes over land use, a scaffold for students to recognize and develop possible actions in current land disputes. This paired assignment provides a structure for students' initial critical reading of Thoreau's work so that they may develop their ideas in context against another text. Ideally, students may choose a more modern text, and they may also choose from any genre, helping students work across time when evaluating the relevance of Thoreau's ideas in the current world. This assignment, again, asks students to consider the specific language used in context in Thoreau's text and then to use comparison and contrast to uncover the more complicated nuances of his use of the term in a rural setting. Variations on this assignment are possible with a change from Thoreau's use of the word *sublime* to his use of hierarchy or his use of binaries as a means of contrasting and clarifying his ideas. Critical rural pedagogy is in play as students are asked to question Thoreau's hierarchies embedded in his fluid use of terms, which holds significance not only for this text but within the larger Romantic movement.

A fourth assignment option asks students, having already generated what the word *sublime* meant for Thoreau (or various things it could mean), to search in contemporary culture or their everyday experiences for moments that either 1) contradict these perceptions or 2) manifest similar ideas. The overall question students may attempt to answer would be how *sublime* might be translated in contemporary or local culture. A journal response that records examples and students' thoughts as they consider these questions would allow them to use their own language and context to explore the intersection of Thoreau's use of the word with their own. Private writing would give students a less risky space in which to question the context of the word. Especially for those students who have strongly opposing views to Thoreau's, having a safe space to work against his statements would support their ability to develop their own, more critical considerations around his assigned each purpose for land use.

A fifth assignment option one might use dives into the famous statement, "I went to the woods to live deliberately" (892), as the starting point for a conversation on the distinction between Thoreau's words on nature/the rural and current interpretations of his words, which may reflect current society's needs rather than the world in which Thoreau created his original work. The in-class assignment asks students to rephrase this paragraph in current language. Working together so that the experiences and expertise of the entire class can be brought into play, the rephrasing may be accomplished as a whole class with a student or teacher scribe to record the rephrasing. A whiteboard, a large piece of paper, or a projected/shared file serves equally well as long as all members of the class can read the developing rephrasing. It is equally workable to have students complete this independently before class and then share their individual versions as the entire group develops a class version on which all can agree. Certainly, Thoreau's idealized vision, which may parallel the rosy past topos, should emerge as part of this activity given Thoreau's perspective. Students will have an opportunity to interrogate Thoreau's philosophy and plans for carrying out a particular type of life. Rather than a formal essay to follow this activity, a private response, a less formal genre, is written by each student, with the prompt, "What was unexpected or what changed in your understanding of this passage after the class discussion?" The personal response allows students to insert their thoughts and perhaps their experiences underlying those ideas.

The sixth activity asks students to consider the way Thoreau's words have been appropriated to represent a connection to unspoiled, unaltered nature. To start this comparison, an internet image search of the phrase "I went to the woods to live deliberately" creates a visual montage. An example screen shot below demonstrates the ways Thoreau's language has been placed in locations, combined with images, or embedded in contemporary artwork.

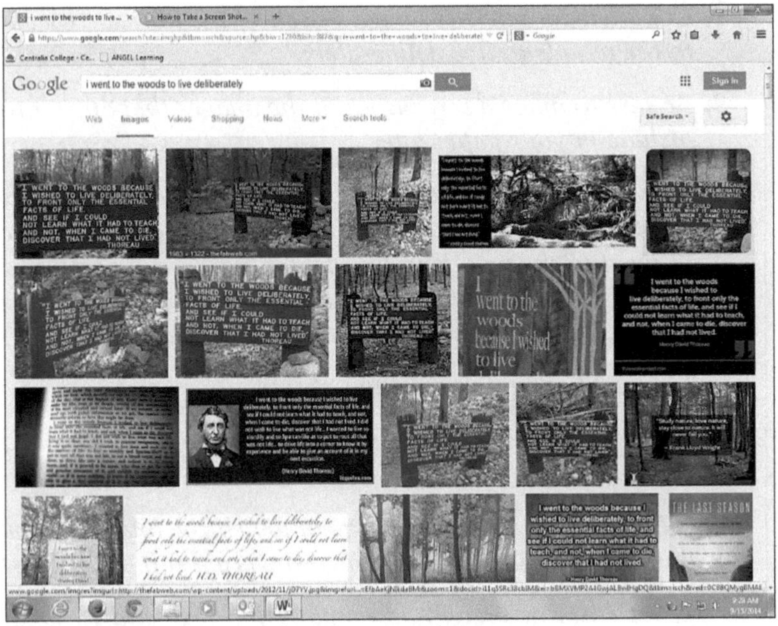

FIGURE 1. *Google Screen Shot, 15 September 2014.*

The ever-shifting nature of image searches allows for a conversation by students that reflects up-to-the-moment interpretations and expressions. This assignment also asks students to first recognize the ways that language is taken up by various people for multiple purposes. The exploration of these images should bring forward the ways language and imagery together alter the perception of Thoreau's initial statement. I have included an assignment sheet below to clarify this assignment.

"I went to the woods to live deliberately."

For this assignment, consider the way Thoreau's words have been appropriated to represent a connection to unspoiled, unaltered nature.

1. *Complete an internet image search of the phrase "I went to the woods to live deliberately."*

2. *Be sure to make a screenshot of the images that appear to include in your paper later.*

3. *Write a short paper (no more than five pages) that compares what Thoreau may have meant when he used the phrase "I went to the woods to live deliberately" in* Walden *and the way the same phrase is used by people in your image search. Be sure to consider the following:*

   Explain Thoreau's use of the phrase.

   Look for patterns in the ways the phrase is represented in the images.

   What are the various contexts in which the images of the phrase exist and how do these contexts affect the meaning?

   What sorts of images accompany the text and to what extent do those images alter your understanding of Thoreau's language?

   What are the messages people are trying to share when they use this quotation from Thoreau, and how are those messages related to the places they include in the images?

   Consider the messages that conservationists present about land and how it is to be used. Do their messages and goals match Thoreau's? To what degree? What other responses to land ownership and use have been obscured or omitted by both Thoreau and conservationists?

This assignment explicitly calls into question how language is used to create a particular vision of how a physical space should be considered by a community. This assignment may bring the tensions embedded in the perspectives and assumptions that underlie both conservationists' idealized vision and the biases of other groups who wish to use land for profitable endeavors. Often in this assignment students note the lack of people in the images. This question of whether there is a lack of human or commercial activity in these images, and how those clash with Thoreau's use of the term, can be explored. There will be students who identify with multiple interests. Students may align with conservation efforts, with agricultural needs, and/or with recreational/tourist uses all at the same time. This assignment reveals these tensions and asks students to grapple with the competing ideas as they are expressed in text, a goal of critical rural pedagogy.

Robert Frost's "Mending Wall"

In Frost's "Mending Wall," there is a common experience that students can use as a starting point for their interactions with the text. Prior to coming to class, students should complete a personal response to the following questions:

What fences have you encountered? Choose one fence from your experiences to consider further. Who built it? Who maintains it? What kinds of fences are there where you live or on the Centralia College campus? What are the purposes of these fences? Have there been any changes to the fences over time? In what ways is the fence a barrier, or, if it is in a liminal space, how does the fence operate as a site of transition?

The purpose of this assignment is to provide students a space to consider the structure of fencing and its purpose in their own lives before exploring Frost's poem. Again, this technique encourages students to bring their own experiences into the classroom as legitimate perspectives to be considered in the discussion and exploration of the poem. Asking rural students to use their experiences as a framework for approaching a text is an important component of critical rural pedagogy. Students will be asked to share both their experiences and their vocabulary around fencing and will then see their work included with equal status to the text, able to serve as a point of comparison with Frost's use of a fence both as a literal object and as a metaphor, helping students develop tactics and skill for critical work that is built around their rural knowledge, a key goal for rural critical pedagogy.

A variation on this activity that will accomplish similar reflections is to present fence imagery in class. Because the stone wall familiar in the northeastern United States is not a universal construction and is certainly unusual in rural Washington State, students may not have seen the type of fence that Frost is referring to in his stone wall imagery. Other professors who use critical rural pedagogy will find they need to make these sorts of adjustments as well. All rural spaces are not homogenous, and these particularities of construction, land use, or means for living in a specific rural space are, of course, part of connecting students at a rural community college with their own understandings of American literature texts. For my students to understand these forms of fences, using projected photographs of northeastern style fences, along with those of fences from other parts of the country, can help students formulate a more complicated sense of how fences might be used. This discussion of context can then transition into a class discussion of the poem. Contextualizing Frost's dominant image then allows students to place their own experiences against this poem, an important aspect of critical pedagogy and especially important for critical rural pedagogy since the generalized fence/wall Frost uses is a familiar construct in rural spaces.

To close out this conversation and to provide an experience in which students find ways to talk, to add to the conversation in the academic setting, I ask students to create a "poetic list" for their conceptions of fences. Poetic lists are collections of images, words, or phrases that are not yet polished or complete. They may function as a form of poetic outline early in the creative, explorative phase of creating a poem. Poetic lists are designed to help students play with language and imagery before they attempt to choose specific portions of these lists, or to make formal revisions of the list, into a recognized poetic form. In this case, I use them to give students a space to play, to explore developing language that is metaphorical and lyrical, or to draw on any number of poetic devices. That allows them to improve their written skills, to increase their appreciation of the difficulties involved in writing poetry, and to develop more critical insights when working with poetry in American literature. I am asking students to explore not only the different connotations of the idea of "fence," but to explore Frost's use of the poetic form by attempting to develop poetic language of their own in response to Frost's original.

Either individually or in pairs, the students choose a fence associated with something important for them, perhaps because of an event that happened around the fence, or because the fence represents a shift or change or border that they have negotiated. They then make a list of images, words, or phrases that they would want to include in their own poem about their fence. Because most students in American literature at Centralia College are not creative writing or English majors, I do not require a formal poem, though some students will choose to use their list to create in a poetic structure. Instead, all students can then share their poetic lists with the class. This way, students have a low-stakes activity that engages their perspectives, provides a platform for sharing the variation and value of their ideas, and helps them to further develop strategies for speaking back against or in more complicating forms than the dominant cultural representations of the rural have allowed for previously.

A fourth activity that may push back against the idea that the rural is simplistic and lacking in value is to do an in-class exegesis of "Mending Wall." Each student starts with a copy of the poem to write on. Line by line, the class discussion walks through the major ideas and structural choices Frost makes in the poem. For example, why is the poem all one stanza? And if traditionally each stanza represents just one idea, does this hold in this poem? What is being suggested by Frost's use of this structure? What are the complications within the poem? Why are there multiple modes of destruction that damage the fence? What is suggested by the specific imagery of the neighbor? The in-class activity can be followed with an essay assignment that encourages students to explore the complications and layers of meaning in the poem.

Students would be asked to address how the poem represents more than one idea at the same time. Students would also be guided to explain the undercurrents in the poem and how they are answered or addressed. Using this more step-by-step approach, students can meet the course outcomes and improve their skills in responding meaningfully to poetry.

The last assignment option that may problematize the poem and connect with students' lives is a multimodal assignment. After we have discussed the poem in class, each student is asked to create a presentation that shows how an image of one object/idea that seems simple may nevertheless be used to represent a personal perspective on a more complicated set of ideas. Ideally, the image must refer to a chore or task the student is familiar with, and each presentation includes images and/or music, as well as written text to explain the student's ideas. The written text may appear in the presentation or may be a written document to accompany the presentation. Critical rural pedagogy suggests that this opportunity to mimic Frost's strategy for compressing complicated ideas into a single image encourages students to think much more critically and to interrogate their own relationships with both the text and their own lives. A student's own work is held in a similar position to Frost's work, highlighting the value of their thoughts, words, and images.

Soliciting students' personal responses, experiences, and perspectives on the poem validates rural students' perspectives in the academic space. If students are also asked to share their work with the rest of the class, each student's voice is also equally attended to. Working in the multimodal form models the importance of these forms in the academic world, again reinforcing the value of rural students' experiences and expertise. This assignment encourages them not only to share but to improve on these skills. Connecting a multimodal form with students' experiences further illustrated the ways that rural people do not lack cultural awareness and technological savvy.

Flannery O'Connor's "Good Country People"

The works of Flannery O'Connor, not often included in high school reading, are generally unfamiliar to first- and second-year college students, and the tone of the stories and the complexity of the characters often take students by surprise. I like to begin with a before-class response to contextualize the discussion for "Good Country People." Students are asked to write a page addressing the following questions and bring it with them to class.

Preparation Questions for O'Connor's "Good Country People"

What does the phrase "good country people" mean to you? Who are the "good" people you know? What makes them good? After you have read it, how do you think "good" is defined in the story?

Since students write their individual responses after they have read the story but before they discuss the story in class, a complicated jumping-off point for discussion should be created. These responses will create a direct refutation of the idea that the rural is limited, as reflected in the idea of the rural as lacking, lagging, and/or just the location of a rosy past. Critical rural pedagogy seeks to give students a chance to work through their own revelations about texts in order to support and value their responses to the dominant culture's accepted representations of the rural. O'Connor's phrase enacts and works against exactly those limitations, assuming that readers will see the minimization of country people embedded in the phrase and the ways it is used in the story.

In class, because students have already committed their initial ideas to paper, the discussion can begin with the following questions: What images, characters, and ideas do you connect with this phrase, and what are the assumptions it draws on? This resulting conversation can be made visible by creating a concept map that both records students' ideas and clarifies those ideas in relation to other ideas presented in class and with a possible hierarchy that is established, reinforced, or rejected by students' interpretations.

Following the discussion, a short in class-activity explores where the phrase appears in O'Connor's short story. The class highlights the phrase in copies of the text, either on paper or on a shared electronic, perhaps projected, document. The character who uses the phrase can be identified, along with the tone and intent of the statement in which it occurs. Students can then write privately, or in a response journal, or have a small-group discussion that encourages them to respond to the hierarchy in these statements. Possible prompting questions for this portion of the activity include these:

As a reader, how do you think of the phrase "good country people"? Does the use of the phrase lead you to elevate or diminish the speaker? When is the phrase "good country people" positive, negative, neutral? What does that say about the general use of the term and how it is used by/for/against specific characters?

The complicated relationships and power structures among the characters may be revealed in the completion of these activities, disputing the ideas of rural places having a rosy past filled with simple people.

A third approach to O'Connor's short story can also be used to show that rural places and people are not adequately represented by the dominant cultural ideas of lack or through the forced lens of a rosy past. An examination of O'Connor's names in particular (Mrs. Freeman, Mrs. Hopewell, Joy/Hulga, Manley Pointer, and Mrs. Freeman's daughters Glynese/Glycerin and Carramae/Caramel) can be a fruitful exercise. A series of columns, each with a character name at its top, can organize students' examination of O'Connor's characters. In each column, students working in pairs can list the details that emerge from the story for each character. Using columns can be a relatively quick way to demonstrate which characters are given more space in the story, and this can serve as a counterpoint to student discussion of the importance of each character in the story as a whole. Once students have their responses mapped out in the columns, they can work next on a closer discussion or analysis of the names of the characters. Are these names that students have encountered before? What does each name reveal or hide about each character? How do these characters compare with real people from our local area? To close the activity, students may be asked to answer the following question "How might the story be categorized: allegory, myth, or cautionary tale? Support your choice with specific examples from the story and your analysis of those examples." This activity allows for students to meet the objectives and course outcomes of the course and encourages students to work through their own understanding of the power dynamics at play in the short story.

When pressed for time in a survey course, another option when reading a short story is to focus on one character. One choice is to examine Joy/Hulga in "Good Country People" and how her interior thoughts and motivations influence the reader's response to what happens to her. When being mindful of critical rural pedagogy, this exploration can look closely at the themes of anti-academic prejudice and intellectual ability that emerge when the young man uses cues to manipulate tradition/culture/manners to take advantage of Joy. Critical rural pedagogy suggests there is another step to take after the class has critiqued this aspect of the tale. How students see their own academic goals reflected back to them in the story, and, more important, to the people in their lives can be a gateway to more complicated thinking. This conversation could take place in small groups, through a number of the tactics Joan Wink has described in *Critical Pedagogy: Notes from the Real World* (2000), e.g.: popcorn, pair-share, or four corners, or in an extended essay. In this situation, it might be fruitful to have students write in pairs or small groups, comparing people's responses to their educational aspirations with one another's and with the response to Joy's advanced degree. A personal written response would finish this exercise with a tangible space in which students can consider their own position in the academic world without needing to share their thoughts with the entire class right away. Instead, they can begin to formulate more thoughtful responses to their own positions within higher education that can be expanded or questioned as they continue through the course.

Alice Walker's "Everyday Use"

Walker's short story pivots on the tension between two sisters, one who has left her rural home to attend college and then live in a city and the other who has stayed on the family's country property. While the daughter who has remained is clearly the "better person," as described by their mother, there is more nuance to the story. Students may have experienced similar tensions. Adding their perspectives can bring these pressures to the surface and enrich the discussion for everyone. The rural home of the protagonist is obviously following the idea of a place that lacks prosperity, advanced education, and cultural awareness, an all-too-familiar representation of the rural. Walker has woven in more complicated understandings of what has importance in this rural context. Her own rural background, as the daughter of sharecroppers in rural Georgia, suggests her access to a more complicated understanding of how the lack and lag of rural places is a misunderstanding by those who do not have rural experiences. Providing students with the space to notice and call out that more layered understanding is important when examining this text. An exploration of "Everyday Use" may leverage students' experiences to sharpen and dig deeper into the distinctions and overlap between urban and rural that are in play in the story.

Prior to reading, a reflection activity focuses students' attention on the way they understand objects, similar to the reference in the title of the story. In private writing or recordings, students are asked to consider objects in their homes that are important—for example, quilts or particular tools. This reflection points their attention to the multiple understandings of objects, especially the value of objects that are in their use, more than their material presence. Students are also asked to consider what makes these objects important. Where did they come from? How have they changed from when they were new?

This reflection is intentionally private. It gives students a draft of ideas from which to draw on during class discussions—not all students are the "quick" thinkers who can dominate a class discussion. This technique also allows students to express their ideas in their own voices, without concern for a polished, finished academic assignment to be turned in. Students are encouraged to bring these reflections with them to class discussion as a starting point for questions or examples they may wish to share or build from. Those students who choose not to share from their reflections will have had a chance to consider their ideas prior to class, and that intellectual work helps to inform their participation in class and to offer a lens through which they consider others' responses to the text. That is important work, too, despite not being made visible in public actions.

The response also directs students to considering the varying meaning of the objects, how their meaning is fluid and dependent on individual perspective. By starting with the importance of these objects, students' experiences with how important an object can be may then help them to align with the way Mama and Maggie feel about the objects in their home. For people who use these objects, there may be significant value in their use in tasks. They may also have a role in memory keeping that is more layered than the derivative "rosy past" despite that perspective, which is often portrayed in images of well-used quilts or old farm equipment hung for display.

In class, a follow-up activity for after students have read the story helps them to articulate these distinctions characters make through objects, revealing something of students' complicated position in the rural-urban binary—is it a false binary when they understand and have a foot in both worlds as community college students? Using a whiteboard, a large piece of paper, or a digital space, I list the objects Walker's characters refer to directly in her story: the butter churn lid, butter churn paddle, house, cow, quilts, kitchen table benches, Grandma's butter dish, and yard. Students then add Mama's and Maggie's statements of value for these objects and Dee's statements. These may be direct quotations from the story, written onto the white space/placeholder, or they may be paraphrases or impressions. Impressions can also be a springboard to interesting interrogations (What makes you say

". . ."?). Encouraging students to use symbols (for example, $), colors, and drawings can give greater latitude to multiple genres of expression, capturing the responses from students who think better in pictures.

This activity may help students see the distinction between the value of these objects to Mama and Maggie as opposed to their value to Dee/Wangero. Dee's character enacts the topos of a rosy past, as well as a lack of worth for these objects in their place of use. This is further complicated by Dee's rural origins and how her adult valuing of objects is purged of her younger self's rural perspective. And how do the objects that are important for students carry additional meaning for them? What are the uses for laptops, books, pens/pencils, bags to carry materials, lab glasses, phones with the LMS app on them? How might these objects also be misunderstood or not seen with the same value by someone who is not a student? The idea here is to connect students with that role more fully. How might my students recognize their parallels to other students in higher education, their friends who have gone to the state universities, or on to graduate school, and perhaps returned as doctors, psychologists, or agronomists for the state extension office?

An alternate activity helps students to notice the contrast Walker draws between the two daughters, Maggie and Dee. At first consideration, Dee is the person who has rejected this rural place and remade herself, but Maggie is also the child who was scarred by fire and unable to move away. The sisters seem to represent a binary, rural and uneducated versus urban and educated, and that is one way to explore the ideas Walker is presenting. But a closer look, with an understanding of what it means, and what it may cost, to exist in both worlds has greater value to my students. It also shows how Walker uses the pull of the dominant topoi to engage readers in what seems familiar but uses that set of ideas to elevate the rural rather than elevate the urban at the expense of the rural. After the class is divided into small groups, each group gets a copy of the story that can be either digitally marked up or physically highlighted. The group then uses a highlighter to mark the text—choose one color for each daughter—marking each phrase or section when Mama talks about or describes each daughter, including their actions. They are asked, "What did you notice that you had not seen before?" Students look for patterns that start to emerge. Initially, they notice which daughter gets the larger share of the text, but they can quickly see the more nuanced distinctions between the two daughters. This activity can be used as a start for a discussion-board conversation, as a statement or shared out to the rest of the class where students can problematize the often-used binary between urban and rural. The daughters can also illustrate the way that individual characters occupy multiple positions of privilege/power/value at the same time.

A fourth possible activity questions the kinds of education and skills that are important and complicates the idea that rural people are lacking in education and abilities. Walker reframes this conversation without denying the differences in what is necessary for success in a poor, rural environment. She includes the prosperous neighboring farm at several points in the story. This pairing again brings in the students' expertise and experiences. How they might talk about themselves becomes a way to define themselves from a positive perspective rather than one of lack, as so often is the case when rural people appear in American literature. Mama's abilities can be the focus for a multimodal assignment.

Mama introduces herself by what she is able to accomplish. How does what she can do equal who she is? Which of those skills and abilities have greater meaning because she is living on a small farm? How do the things she can do relate to what she needs to do to live well in this place? If you were to introduce yourself that way, what would you say? What can you do because of where and how you have lived so far?

After class discussion of the fifth paragraph of the story, using the framing above, students are asked to make their introductions more formal. They may introduce themselves, or they may introduce someone they know (classmate, family members, co-worker, neighbor). Introduction needs to be brief, similar to Mama's introduction, and include an audio file. That audio file may be music, or the person being introduced speaking, or the student reading that text. Only one PowerPoint, Prezi, or Google slide can be used, and there must be one image. That image may be the person or may be something about that person (where they live/work, objects they use). These limitations are intended to help students compress their introduction in the way Walker has done for Mama, so that they say more to the audience than just the limited number of words (no more than 150) suggests. These introductions can be shared in class or, more typically, submitted to a discussion board in a learning management system so that students can share their work with one another outside of class time. While watching one another's introductions, students can compile a list of the important skills and knowledge they observe, which we can discuss in class. The opportunity to explore Walker's use of precise imagery and how that influences the reader's perceptions of Mama is combined with students' mimicking that move, creating precise images that point out what is useful and valuable in the person they have selected. As usual, I include my own introduction in the shared portion.

Doing the assignments with my students helps me to see the glitches in the assignments but also provides an example. I often share the creative portion of completing work—drafts of my own work become examples for how to work through those moments when an idea is not coming together, when a draft is not going well, how to regroup, how to revel in what is working, how to ask for help when needed. Working cooperatively is encouraged. As a class, we discuss what sorts of audio files would be helpful for this assignment. Student expertise is always included, welcomed, and valued, I hope reinforcing their importance in the academic space at the college and other institutions of higher education where they may continue their studies.

A fifth possible activity focuses on how "Everyday Use" includes an overt discussion of the racial tensions at the time. Mama briefly relates a side story to explain why she can't imagine looking a white man in the eye except in her TV dream; the

Black farmers down the road had their cattle poisoned by white neighbors, and they then stood armed with guns—why is this important enough to include but not given a larger portion of the story? What is the audience expected to understand without more explanation? Students can write or record an initial informal response to this episode, considering the following: what makes the response of the neighbors whose cows were poisoned more than a passing detail here? What is Walker making sure we see but with a different twist—they fought back, they armed themselves. Walker does not tell us what the outcome of the confrontation was, so does that suggest that no more cows were poisoned? How do people solve similar problems when the community does not value them or when calling the police or the sheriff may not help them?

My last suggestion for this story focuses on the fact that Dee went away to college. Rural students are in a unique position at this moment in their lives, both as members of a community that has a complicated relationship with higher education and as students who are engaged in that exact endeavor. Does becoming a more educated person separate them from their larger community in ways that are not repairable, as the topos of the rosy past would suggest? Can they be both full members of their home communities and aware of the larger world?

I would argue yes, and I am hoping they will see the same fault line in Walker's story—Walker herself was educated at Spelman and at Sarah Lawrence. She had a highly regarded higher educational experience, certainly seen as much higher in status than that of my community college students.

Again, using highlighters and the original text, this time the class goes through the story together, pointing out sections that illustrate what the problem is with the things that Dee knows compared to what Mama and Maggie know. A whole-class discussion can then be woven into this group analysis. What would have happened if Dee had brought the rural knowledge with her to college? How does she "pass" for not rural? What is the reason the two sisters represent two completely different lives, and the rural sister is clearly, at least in Mama's eyes, and ours as we learn her perspective, the better, the more content of the two sisters? What are the nuances of what Dee wants when she returns—to turn the objects into museum pieces, representations of things, rather than usable things? After the discussion, having the students write or record a private reflection provides an opportunity to consider their positions in higher education. Considering their goals in light of a rural community college experience is important for recognizing the value of their experiences and voices in higher education.

Summary Thoughts

In this chapter, I have developed the context in which American literature is taught on my campus, and that may parallel the situations at other small, rural community colleges. It is my hope that the activities that I have developed and shared in this chapter will serve as a starting point for inserting a more critical rural pedagogy into the classroom experiences of my students. I believe that these activities can be used in other rural community colleges, and the larger ideas of a critical rural pedagogy are here illustrated in a way that other professors and instructors can make use of these pedagogical moves in ways that have resonance and usefulness in their individual situations. As stated before, critical rural pedagogy aims to accept and problematize students' use of language in relation to their rural experiences, to give students opportunities to develop tactics and skills that helps them make use of their rural knowledge, and to explore the context in which rural students find themselves as simultaneous members of multiple groups with varying degrees of power within the dominant culture, in rural locations, and as undergraduates. I turn now to my final chapter, where I will outline possible next steps that I and other teachers and scholars may explore in the future.

Chapter Four

Reaching the Goal: Rural Students Move On

This book began when I first confronted a disconnect between what I believed a small subset of my rural students should and would want to share in my American literature classes and the reality of what they were willing to share. It was only upon further reflection and study that I began to realize that the difficulty had multiple causes. First, I was focusing on only one small portion of my rural students, those who had direct experience with life on a farm, or with animal husbandry, or with ranching. I was overlooking the totality of experiences that all of my students bring to the classroom, the tremendous variety of perspectives they contribute. I was also assuming that the experiences they brought with them from their K–12 education would be somewhat consistent, relying on an implied set of rural literacies and pedagogies. However, I learned that a mutually agreed-upon set of rural literacies and pedagogical practices was not the case. Second, I was overlooking the three consistently recurring topoi that could be used in my classroom, the idea of the rural as a place of lack, and/or lag, and/or a slice of a rosy past. Because these topoi circulate variably and widely in our literature, public discourse, and everyday lives, they offer powerful access points for critique, reflection, local connections, and possibly action and intervention for my students. Third, I was attempting to use critical pedagogy, but I learned that there are substantial aspects of critical pedagogy that are not useful or accurate when applied to classrooms in rural community colleges. As this project developed, I discovered the gaps between what I believed and classroom reality. Students did not fit into a stark binary of powerful-powerless or privileged-not privileged. More typically, they occupied multiple positions in a hegemonic structure, sometimes concurrently and sometimes moving between positions depending on current context. These identifiable gaps between my expectations and my students' expectations would lead me to develop a critical rural pedagogy.

It is my hope that the insights I have uncovered and this critical rural pedagogy are useful not only in my present teaching situation, but for other instructors of American literature working in similar rural community college settings. This work may also apply to those who are teaching in parallel spaces, e.g., rural students in classes across multiple locations—college in high school, Advanced Placement high school classes, private colleges, and regional universities.

Vignette: Graduation Celebration

Each spring, Centralia's graduation takes place on the lawn in the center of the main campus. There is a raised dais and folding chairs are set out on the lawn in a radiating pattern. Faculty and students typically take up chairs closest to the temporary stage, and another couple of hundred people fill the remaining chairs. Behind, there are family members and friends who were not able to arrive early enough to snag a folding chair. There are no tickets for our graduation. Instead, an invitation is extended to all who wish to attend. That also means that the back of the lawn is filled with small children playing games of hide-and-seek, tag, or peek-a-boo throughout the ceremony. Families arrive in large and at times astonishing numbers. All the cousins come when a student is the first in the family to graduate from college. There are whoops of joy as students' names are called and equivalent celebrations for students completing high school programs, professional certificates, associate degrees, and applied bachelor of sciences degrees.

But what happens after these students receive their diplomas? How might we support those students who have just completed their courses of study in ways that will allow and encourage them to move on to their next goal?

Some Centralia College graduates will begin working in the community with their new licenses or credentials. A subset of graduates will return to Centralia College in the future to extend their higher education into associate degrees or a Bachelor of Applied Science degree. Other graduates will transfer into programs at universities and private colleges where they will complete bachelor's degrees. Additionally, there are students who have not completed a degree, instead having taken several transfer-level courses, who then move on to university without completing their associates' degrees.

Out of all these successful, rural community college students, a small percentage will have taken the American literature survey offered at Centralia College. It is my hope that the information, theory, and practices I have developed will in some small way have helped them not only to have successfully completed my course, but also to leave our campus with an improved skill set for participating in the next phase of their academic and professional lives.

Critical rural pedagogy is a tool that can push back against the dominant culture's assumptions about the value of rural spaces, which students have often internalized. Students then have points of tactical leverage, helping them to make their understandings of texts in American literature more complex. On a larger scale, these interventions may provide a stable connection to their important place in higher education. Rural students who build on their skills and unique knowledge have a more nuanced understanding and ability to complicate the flat perceptions of the rural as a place of lack, lag, or a fictional rosy past, which they will encounter as they transfer to universities and operate in the dominant culture. The time between when a student first enters an American literature course and when they complete the course is the focus of my book. However, it is also important to me that students have experiences in the academic classroom that encourage them to see themselves as relevant and important contributors to higher education.

Catching Up with Alexis

In summer 2021, I was able to follow up with Alexis, the example student from Chapter 1 who illustrated my need for a more complicated, nuanced understanding of rural students. Alexis had grown up on a small property outside of town where she raised rabbits for show. She completed her associate degree at Centralia College and transferred to Western Washington University in Bellingham. After completing her bachelor's degree, she worked for a short time at Centralia College in the e-learning department. This is not an unusual pattern. Quite a number of our current staff and faculty are former students. She then applied to graduate school in Illinois, where she completed her master's degree in student services. Since then, she has worked as a residence director, training and supporting the resident assistants (RAs) along with developing programming for students who live on campus. Her first position was with the University of Minnesota at Duluth, a branch campus that she described as "rural [and] less academically rigorous" (Austin) than the main campus, located in Minneapolis–St. Paul. She enjoyed her work there. She described Duluth, population under 80,000, as living "in the city because I was on the college campus" (Austin).

After two years in Duluth, she switched to the main campus. She commented that the Twin Cities campus felt different, pointing out that the variation was due in part to the University's R1 status; doctoral-granting and research-focused university goals invite more academically advanced students who match the research university model. Alexis commented on the change in how she perceived the bigger campus: "At Twin Cities, [I feel] so much more detached [from the local community], [and campus] politics [are] more dominant than at Duluth" (Austin). She also pointed explicitly to an important geographic difference, where one "can literally do all you need within a block" (Austin). Additionally, Alexis described this as being "far from my experience from Centralia College" because the university has 50,000 students compared to Centralia's typical 1,800 students attending each year (Austin).

Alexis has made a professional life within higher education. She knows that she has an important role to fulfill within higher education, in part because of her experiences growing up in a rural space. Interestingly, her answers to my questions demonstrate how her rural background is both revealed and obscured. Her response to my question: *How does your rural self exist in this space? What do you submerge to "pass" for urban?* reflects the nuanced existence of a person who began in a rural space but now lives in a major city. She exemplifies the multiple positions she inhabits as factors of geography, population density, and time. She laughed as she replied:

> No. I am in an overwhelming metropolis—I was raised rural, but I am no longer a rural human—urban, but not happy about it. There are just so many people here. This is the biggest place I will ever live. I want to go back to about 80,000 population. I miss the small community/knowing everyone and their histories. (Austin)

Alexis's connection to her rural home remains important. She returns to the rural property where her parents continue to live at least once a year to visit them and to spend time with her friends in the area. Her discomfort in her new surroundings is complicated by her desire to continue working as a residence director, work she describes as fulfilling and important. Not surprisingly, she continues to bring her sensibilities toward community and connection from her rural upbringing, and she understands transfer students. Specifically, she has a desire to see them supported in her work, again, in part because of her own experiences. She spoke of ways her voice in university conversations helps a range of students, including rural students who are often transfer students living in the on-campus residences.

Alexis continues to use her rural experiences as a reference when speaking with me about her current life in Minneapolis—reflecting her roots in Lewis County, Washington, where we have a shared set of reference points.

> Usually, 7,500 [are] living on campus, larger than most towns in Lewis County. The building I supervise is [the size of] my [high school] graduating class times three. It is so much harder

> to build relationships. At Centralia I knew faculty I had never had a class with and I knew them, but I don't even know the people in a single department here. Here, neighborhoods mean so much, [and this is] complicated by me living on campus so I don't get to interact with my neighbors. (Austin)

Alexis's connection to higher education is complicated by two factors. She clearly sees a place where she can contribute to her chosen field, but that requires living in an urban space. Generally, rural community colleges do not have residence halls, so though she would like to return to a rural area where the community ties are more visible, active, and overlapping across families and locations, that is not a viable option. She explains: "[I] still definitely want to stay in residence, so the next best option is a four-year college that will provide housing for CC [community college] students" (Austin).

A second factor is that she sees a particular role for herself in that urban university space: "[I] also enjoyed supervising upper-[division] housing that has more transfer students. I love them in part because we don't support them as well as we should" (Austin). She aligns with the experiences of transfer students, who often started in community college settings. She sees her own experience as a transfer student as a lens through which she can advocate for students who do not fit the traditional pattern of the eighteen-to-twenty-year-old, straight-from-high-school student, who left home for an R1 university. Not surprisingly, given the pressures of internalized ideas about the rural in dominant culture, she does not highlight her rural experiences. Instead, she focuses on the transfer experience, with her own rural background quietly under the surface of her current work and future plans.

Critical Rural Pedagogy: Where Do We Go from Here?

My book's aim has been to clarify and develop a more focused definition of rural literacy that builds on Kim Donehower, Charlotte Hogg, and Eileen E. Schell's work in *Rural Literacies* and that can be deployed as part of a critical rural pedagogy that is useful and theoretically sound for rural students. Specifically,

I've focused on a pedagogy developed for first- and second-year college students attending rural colleges who are enrolled in American literature classes. I have also developed a theoretical approach to working with students in my rural community college. While this work emerged from literature courses taught in a rural community college in Washington State, the insights of this book are applicable and can be adapted for other professors in rural community colleges and teaching in rural contexts more generally. I hope that rural students who may not have seen themselves as full members of the scholarly community of higher education may have a more complicated understanding of their importance as members of the academy and as full participants who should bring their rural experiences with them into higher education.

Because of the invisibility of rural people and issues in most college classrooms, my rural community college students crystallized a point of intervention for me, and this book has been my attempt to begin to close gaps in understanding the myriad experiences of rural students and the pedagogical practices that might be attuned to their needs. The space between these students' experiences and the representations of the rural they encounter provides a lever that allows them to draw on their expertise, to see themselves in the curriculum, and to reveal the constructed nature of the representations of the rural encountered in American literature texts. It is my hope that those students who have taken my American literature course will have developed not only an ability to discuss and analyze literature, but also to speak with some confidence in an academic classroom. It is also my hope that my project has enabled some of these students to practice bringing their expertise as rural students to other locations in higher education.

There is theory and practice explored in this book that can be useful beyond the boundaries of my classroom and my campus. The example course assignments I present in Chapter 3 are intended to be picked up by other professors of American literature teaching in similarly geographically isolated community colleges. These exercises are a sampling of activities and assignments for other instructors to build upon, and I expect conversations about developing activities to appear in the regional two-year college English conferences.

For instructors and professors working with rural students across the country, my work has made visible several points of tension. Most important, the need to work with rural students who concurrently occupy multiple spaces of power along a continuum of hierarchy necessitates a variation on critical pedagogy. As I have conceived it, a critical rural pedagogy creates a space in which these students' multiple positions are not an impediment to their learning. Instead, their ability to work from multiple perspectives of power and marginalization leads to a richer, more complex classroom environment. Additionally, by using a critical rural pedagogy, rural students may be empowered, may increase their skills with language, and, I hope, may find a stronger sense of their importance and connection in the larger world of higher education. Although I have demonstrated ways to use critical rural pedagogy in an American literature course, these same principles can and, I would argue, should be used in related language and cultural disciplines. Just a few courses of study that can utilize critical rural pedagogy include composition, literary studies, language studies, humanities, and sociology. This book begins a conversation that needs more research and contextual perspectives from my colleagues at community colleges and other institutions of higher education whose students work within parallel constraints.

Another point of tension my work has identified and grappled with is the ambiguous and variable use of the terms *rural literacy* and *rural pedagogy*. While my book has taken an initial stride toward defining these ideas without reifying the conception of the rural in monolithic terms, more research needs to be done on creating consensus or perhaps developing more finely tuned terminology to gain a better sense of how rural literacy and rural pedagogy may interact, both controlling and altering the spaces they attempt to describe. It is critically important to me to determine the validity of my theorizing around critical rural pedagogy. Scholars in the field of composition and literature pedagogy may also pursue research that examines the boundaries of a critical rural pedagogy and its implications for rural students because my work has established an area of substudy that has not yet been fully developed. I look forward to contributing to this work, but I also value the perspectives other scholars will bring to this developing theory and the application of critical rural pedagogy in the classroom.

Although no one course, no one set of experiences, can accomplish all of the goals I have set, I have developed first steps toward enriching students' classroom experiences via a critical rural pedagogy and by expanding my theorizing so that others can engage critical rural pedagogical practices and make use of these concepts in the construction of their classes and programs in rural community colleges. In summary, critical rural pedagogy foregrounds rural students' experiences across multiple contexts of power and powerlessness, building on their own language in an academic setting, which is then used by students to speak back against limiting representations of the rural. This context allows for students to improve their skills in and around their own and others' language, resulting in students who are more empowered and connected to their value within higher education. While I believe my work makes strides toward the goals I set for my students, for my own professional growth, and for other teachers interested in pursuing such goals, there are quite a number of next steps that I would like to explore after the completion of this book. My work up to this point illuminates numerous features of study that require further attention.

I envision several directions for future study that I and others may pick up. My work is centered on students' context in and around Centralia College, which has a student body that is predominantly white, economically challenged, and first-generation. Because my initial theorizing around critical rural pedagogy is grounded in an overtly rural context, there is an area of alignment with other scholars who interrogate students' geographical locations in pedagogical work. How might a detailed examination of rural community colleges located farther from urban centers or that operate as branch campuses for universities complicate and contest critical rural pedagogy? How might the perspectives that scholars from collections like *Relations, Locations, Positions: Composition Theory for Writing Teachers*, edited by Peter Vandenberg, Sue Hum, and Jennifer Clary-Lemon, problematize my theorizing?

While I have touched on the concerns of students of color, the discussion presented is merely superficial; my acknowledgment of the multiple layers of marginalization of these students is insufficient. As Aja Martinez points out in *Counterstory: The Rhetoric and Writing of Critical Race Theory*, the framework of critical race theory is a centrally important methodology, and her call that "[e]ducators should work from a premise that racism is prevalent in American society in general, and in education in particular" (112) makes clear avenues for further research and scholarship around critical rural pedagogy. Her important thread is beyond the scope of this first theorizing work, yet her call to make racism central to the work of educators needs attention going forward. Additionally, the systemic nature of educational biases of race, gender, ableness, and class present further lenses through which to conceptualize the concept of "rural student." How might an explicitly intersectional approach to critical rural pedagogy improve its value for students?

A third research perspective to take up in the future is to further understand the ways in which critical rural pedagogy may alter a student's relationship with their own community. It may be important to interrogate the truism "that which observes, alters." What are the implications for students who approach American literature texts by pushing back against the fictional, flat, or backward representations those texts create of the rural? Might these students respond to a fractured view of the rural with questions of their own identities as rural people? What does it mean when students like Alexis describe themselves as "no longer rural"? What are not only the possible benefits but the complications created for students when the distinctions between how the dominant culture defines "rural" and how their experiences are made explicit?

Parting Thoughts

As presented in the previous section, I am convinced that the work I have begun here can serve as a springboard for continued professional scholarship. As discussed above, the complications of working with a student population that has not yet been studied in detail leads to multiple possible projects. The crossroads between American literature, representations of the rural, and critical rural pedagogy, at this early point in the work, is a space in the scholarly conversation that has not yet been fully outlined, let alone explored and thoroughly examined by scholars and teaching professionals. I find myself at a fascinating intersection. One foot is firmly in the community college world of literature instruction, and the other foot is planted in the need for research to further develop both theories and practices that will inform work with rural community college students in American literature classes. I happily anticipate beginning these explorations and am hopeful that others will join me in this work.

Works Cited

"About Centralia College." Centralia College, 2018, www.centralia.edu/about.

"About Our District." Napavine School District, 18 October 2014, www.napa.k12/wa.us/aboutus.aspx.

Abrams, Robert E. *Landscape and Ideology in American Renaissance Literature: Topographies of Skepticism*. Cambridge UP, 2004.

Allen, Ricky Lee, and César Augusto Rossatto. "Does Critical Pedagogy Work with Privileged Students?" *Teacher Education Quarterly*, vol. 36, no. 1, Winter 2009, pp. 163–80.

Aristotle. *On Rhetoric: A Theory of Civic Discourse*. Translated by George A. Kennedy, Oxford UP, 2007.

Austin, Alexis. Interview. Conducted by Sharon Mitchler, 15 July 2021.

Bartholomae, David. "Inventing the University." *Cross-Talk in Comp Theory: A Reader*, edited by Victor Villanueva, Jr., NCE, 1997, pp. 589–620.

Batteau, Allen. *The Invention of Appalachia*. U of Arizona P, 1990.

Baym, Nina, editor. *The Norton Anthology of American Literature*. Shorter 7th edition, W. W. Norton, 2008.

Berry, Wendell. *The Art of the Commonplace: The Agrarian Essays of Wendell Berry*. Edited by Norman Wirzba, Counterpoint, 2002.

Bredahl, A. Carl. *New Ground: Western American Narrative and the Literary Canon*. U of North Carolina P, 1989.

Brickhouse, Anna. *Transamerican Literary Relations and the Nineteenth-Century Public Sphere*. Cambridge UP, 2004.

Brückner, Martin, and Hsuan L. Hsu. Introduction. *American Literary Geographies: Spatial Practice and Cultural Production, 1500–1900*, edited by Brückner and Hsu, U of Delaware P, 2007.

Burke, Kenneth. *Language as Symbolic Action: Essays on Life, Literature, and Method.* U of California P, 1966.

Canagarajah, A. Suresh. *Literacy as Translingual Practice: Between Communities and Classrooms.* Routledge, 2013.

Centralia College, *Year One Report.* 14 September 2011, www.centralia.edu › admin › accreditation › year-one_self-study_sept2011.

"The Centralia College Mission." Centralia College, www.centralia.edu/about/mission.aspx.

Cintron, Ralph. "Democracy and Its Limitations." *The Public Work of Rhetoric: Citizen-Scholars and Civic Engagement*, edited by John M. Ackerman and David J. Coogan, U of South Carolina P, 2010, pp. 98–116.

Comer, Krista. *Landscapes of the New West: Gender and Geography in Contemporary Women's Writing.* U of North Carolina P, 1999.

"Common Course Numbering." *Washington State Board for Community and Technical Colleges.* www.sbctc.edu/colleges-staff/programs-services/common-course-numbering/ccn.

Corkery, Caleb. "Rhetoric of Race: Critical Pedagogy without Resistance." *Teaching English in the Two-Year College*, vol. 36, no. 3, Mar. 2009, pp. 224–56.

Crowley, Sharon, and Debra Hawhee. *Ancient Rhetorics for Contemporary Students.* 4th edition, Pearson Longman, 2009.

Davidson, Osha Gray. *Broken Heartland: The Rise of America's Rural Ghetto.* Expanded edition, U of Iowa P, 1996.

de Certeau, Michel. *The Practice of Everyday Life.* U of California P, 1984.

Donehower, Kim, Charlotte Hogg, and Eileen E. Schell, editors. *Reclaiming the Rural: Essays on Literacy, Rhetoric, and Pedagogy.* Southern Illinois UP, 2012.

———. *Rural Literacies.* Southern Illinois UP, 2007.

Edmondson, Jacqueline. *Prairie Town: Redefining Rural Life in the Age of Globalization.* Rowman and Littlefield, 2003.

"Faculty and Staff Data." Centralia College, Institutional Research, Student Information and Demographics, www.centralia.edu/about/leadership/institutional-research/.

Fast Facts 2022. American Association of Community Colleges, www.aacc.nche.edu/research-trends/fast-facts/.

Fishman, Andrea. *Amish Literacy: What and How it Means*. Heinemann, 1988.

Fleming, David. *City of Rhetoric: Revitalizing the Public Sphere in Metropolitan America*. SUNY P, 2008.

Frazier, Ian. *Great Plains*. Farrar, Straus and Giroux, 1989.

Freire, Paulo. *Pedagogy of the Oppressed*. Penguin Books, 1972.

Frost, Robert. "Mending Wall." McMichael and Leonard, pp. 1539–40.

Giroux, Henry A. "Academic Freedom under Fire: The Case for Critical Pedagogy." *College Literature*, vol. 33, no. 4, Fall 2006, pp. 1–42.

Gjelten, Thomas. "Elk River, Idaho: The Pursuit of Quality Schooling in a Threatened Community." Nachtigal, pp. 207–26.

———. "Gary, Texas: The Rise of *Loblolly*." Nachtigal, pp. 227–46.

Graff, Gerald, and Cathy Birkenstein. *They Say / I Say: The Moves That Matter in Academic Writing*. 2nd edition, W. W. Norton, 2010.

Guerra, Juan C. "Life in the Neither/Nor: Figural Representations of Literacy, Space and Identity." The Working Papers Series on Negotiating Differences in Language and Literacy. U of Louisville, 2012.

Haas, Toni, and Paul M. Nachtigal. *Place Value: An Educator's Guide to Good Literature on Rural Lifeways, Environments, and Purposes of Education*. ERIC Clearinghouse on Rural Education and Small Schools, 1998.

Hautecoeur, Jean-Paul. "Opening Reflections: Literacy in Rural Areas—Orientations for Action Research." *Alpha 94: Literacy and Cultural Development Strategies in Rural Areas*, edited by Hautecoeur, Culture Concepts, 1994, pp. 7–24.

Hogg, Charlotte. "Beyond Agrarianism: Toward a Critical Pedagogy of Place." Donehower et al., *Rural Literacies*, pp. 120–54.

hooks, bell. *Talking Back: Thinking Feminist, Thinking Black*. South End Press, 1989.

Kaye/Kantrowitz, Melanie. "Representation, Entitlement, and Voyeurism: Teaching across Difference." *Twenty-First-Century*

Feminist Classrooms: Pedagogies of Identity and Difference, edited by Amie A. Macdonald and Susan Sánchez-Casal, Palgrave Macmillan, 2002, pp. 281–98.

Kincheloe, Joe L. *Critical Pedagogy Primer*. Peter Lang, 2004.

———. *Knowledge and Critical Pedagogy: An Introduction*. Springer, 2008.

Kopelson, Karen. "Rhetoric on the Edge of Cunning; Or, the Performance of Neutrality (Re)considered as a Composition Pedagogy for Student Resistance." *College Composition and Communication*, vol. 55, no. 1, Sept. 2003, pp. 115–46.

Lauter, Paul, general editor. *Heath Anthology of American Literature, Volume B: Early Nineteenth Century, 1800–1865*. 6th edition, Wadsworth Cengage Learning, 2009.

———, general editor. *Heath Anthology of American Literature, Volume D: Modern Period, 1910–1945*. 6th edition, Wadsworth Cengage Learning, 2009.

———, general editor. *Heath Anthology of American Literature, Volume E: Contemporary Period, 1945 to the Present*. 6th edition, Wadsworth Cengage Learning, 2009.

"Lewis County." United States Census, www.census.gov/quickfacts/fact/table/lewiscountywashington,WA/PST045219.

Lowe, Peggy. "Farmers and Their Cooperative Settle Lawsuit on Fixing the Price of Milk." *The Salt: What's on Your Plate*, National Public Radio, 23 Jan. 2013.

Martinez, Aja Y. *Counterstory: The Rhetoric and Writing of Critical Race Theory*. CCCC/NCTE, 2020.

Marx, Leo. *The Machine in the Garden: Technology and the Pastoral Ideal in America*. Oxford UP, 1964.

Mathieu, Paula. *Tactics of Hope: The Public Turn in English Composition*. Boynton/Cook Publishers, 2005.

Matthiessen, F. O. Introduction. *American Renaissance: Art and Expression in the Age of Emerson and Whitman*. Oxford UP, 1941, pp. vii–xvi.

McComiskey, Bruce, and Cynthia Ryan, editors. *City Comp: Identities, Spaces, Practices*. SUNY P, 2003.

McMichael, George, and James S. Leonard, editors. *Concise Anthology of American Literature*. 6th edition, Pearson Prentice Hall, 2006.

Mulholland, Valerie. "For All Students in This Place." Donehower et al., *Reclaiming*, pp. 190–206.

Nachtigal, Paul M., editor. *Rural Education: In Search of a Better Way*. Westview Press, 1982.

———. "Theme V: Accepting Rural Reality." Nachtigal, pp. 301–12.

O'Connor, Flannery. "Good Country People." Lauter, *Volume E: Contemporary Period, 1945 to the Present*, pp. 2567–78.

Orr, David W. "Re-ruralizing Education." *Rooted in the Land: Essays on Community and Place*, edited by William Vitek and Wes Jackson, Yale UP, 1996, pp. 226–34.

Petrosky, Anthony. "Rural Poverty and Literacy in the Mississippi Delta: Dilemmas, Paradoxes, and Conundrums." *The Right to Literacy*, edited by Andrea A. Lunsford, Helene Moglen, and James Slevin, MLA, 1990, pp. 61–73.

Pollan, Michael. *The Omnivore's Dilemma: A Natural History of Four Meals*. Penguin Press, 2006.

Popper, Deborah E., and Frank J. Popper. "The Buffalo Commons: Metaphor as Method." *Geographical Review*, vol. 89, no. 4, Oct. 1999, pp. 491–510.

"Population, Table 4." *United States Census Bureau*, 27 Aug. 1993, www.census.gov/population/censusdata/table-4.pdf. Accessed 13 Aug. 2012.

Pratt, Mary Louise. *Imperial Eyes: Travel Writing and Transculturation*. 2nd edition, Routledge, 2008.

Rai, Candice. *Democracy's Lot: Rhetoric, Publics, and the Places of Invention*. U of Alabama P, 2016.

Reid, Alexander. "Free Action or Resistance: Cultural Critique in the Classroom." *Theory and Event*, vol. 4, no. 3, 2000.

Reynnells, Louise, and Patricia LaCaille John, editors. "What Is Rural?" Revised and updated Sept. 2008, United States Department of Agriculture, National Agricultural Library, Rural Information Center, www.nal.usda.gov/ric/ricpubs/what_is_rural.shtml. Accessed 19 July 2009.

Robbins, Ted. "Fla. Tomato Growers Say Mexico Trade Deal Is Rotten." *Morning Edition*, National Public Radio, 23 Jan. 2013.

Smith, Henry Nash. *Virgin Land: The American West as Symbol and Myth*. Vintage Books, 1957.

Sohn, Katherine Kelleher. *Whistlin' and Crowin' Women of Appalachia: Literacy Practices since College*. Southern Illinois UP, 2006.

"Student Demographics." Centralia College, Institutional Research, Student Information and Demographics, www.centralia.edu/about/leadership/institutional-research/.

Theobald, Paul. *Teaching the Commons: Place, Pride, and the Renewal of Community*. Westview Press, 1997.

Thoreau, Henry David. "Where I Lived and What I Lived For." Baym, pp. 886–96.

Tinberg, Howard, and Jean-Paul Nadeau. *The Community College Writer: Exceeding Expectations*. Southern Illinois UP, 2010.

Trainor, Jennifer Seibel. "Critical Pedagogy's 'Other': Constructions of Whiteness in Education for Social Change." *College Composition and Communication*, vol. 53, no. 4, June 2002, pp. 631–50.

TYCA Two-Year College Facts and Data Report, 2005. Two-Year College English Association, National Council of Teachers of English.

Vandenberg, Peter, Sue Hum, and Jennifer Clary-Lemon, editors. *Relations, Locations, Positions: Composition Theory for Writing Teachers*. NCTE, 2006.

Walker, Alice. "Everyday Use." McMichael and Leonard, pp. 2014–11.

"W. F. West High School Overview." Best High Schools, *USA Today*, 19 Oct. 2014, www.usnews.com/education/best-high-schools/washington/districts/chehalis-school-district/w-f-west-high-school-20784

Wilder, Laura, and Joanna Wolfe. "Sharing the Tacit Rhetorical Knowledge of the Literary Scholar: The Effect of Making Disciplinary Conventions Explicit in Undergraduate Writing about Literature Courses." *Research in the Teaching of English*, vol. 44, no. 2, Nov. 2009, pp. 174–204.

Wink, Joan. *Critical Pedagogy: Notes from the Real World*. 2nd edition, Longman, 2000.

Works Cited

W. K. Kellogg Foundation. *Perceptions of Rural America*, 9 Dec. 2002, wkkf.issuelab.org/resource/perceptions-of-rural-america.html.

———. "Perceptions of Rural America: Congressional Perspectives." 3 May 2002. Web. Accessed 21 June 2011.

Zencey, Eric. "The Rootless Professors." *Rooted in the Land: Essays on Community and Place*, edited by William Vitek and Wes Jackson, Yale UP, 1996, pp. 15–19.

Index

Author

Sharon Mitchler is professor of English and humanities at Centralia College. Mitchler teaches a range of undergraduate courses in composition, literature, humanities, ethics, and film. Her current research focuses on critical rural pedagogy and teaching for transfer. Mitchler's scholarship has been published in *Teaching English in the Two-Year College* and *Composition Studies*. She is a former national chair of the Two-Year College English Association.

This book was typeset in Sabon.
Typefaces used on the cover include Bakersville Old Face,
Helvetica Neue LT Std, and Abril Titling Cnd Sb.
The book was printed on 50-lb. white offset paper.